Light
on the
Path

Light on the *Path*

Guiding Symbols
for Insight and Discernment

Meeting God through Dreams, Sacraments, Stories,
Meditation, and Spiritual Practice

Daniel L. Prechtel

 Morehouse Publishing
NEW YORK

Unless otherwise noted, the Scripture quotations contained herein are from the New Revised Standard Version Bible, copyright © 1989 by the Division of Christian Education of the National Council of Churches of Christ in the U.S.A. Used by permission. All rights reserved.

"Song to My Other Self" © 2007 Elsie Landstrom. Used by permission.

Morehouse Publishing, 19 East 34th Street, New York, NY 10016

Morehouse Publishing is an imprint of Church Publishing Incorporated.
www.churchpublishing.org

Cover design by Jenn Kopec, 2Pug Design
Typeset by John Turnbull

Library of Congress Cataloging-in-Publication Data

Prechtel, Daniel L., author.
    Light on the path : guiding symbols for insight and discernment :
        meeting God through dreams, sacraments, stories, meditation, and spiritual
        practice / Daniel L. Prechtel.
    New York : Morehouse Publishing, 2016. | Includes bibliographical references.
            LCCN 2016019855 (print) | LCCN 2016031270 (ebook) |
            ISBN 9780819232953 (pbk.) | ISBN 9780819232960 (ebook)
        Spiritual life—Christianity. | Christian art and symbolism. |
        Discernment (Christian theology)
    BV4501.3 .P736 2016 (print) | BV4501.3 (ebook)
    248.4/6—dc23

LC record available at https://lccn.loc.gov/2016019855

Printed in the United States of America

Contents

Chapter 4: Contexts for Discernment and Guiding Symbols

Chapter 5: Participating in God's Dream

Acknowledgments

I AM INDEBTED to a "whole company of saints" who gave me their valuable time in reading over various iterations of this book and generously sharing their thoughts and suggestions, helping it to completion. Duncan Burns, Sue Nebel, Will Westerfield, and Philip Ayers all made valuable contributions in the early stages of development. Dwight Judy lent his support and encouragement as an esteemed spiritual guide, author, and educator. Diane Stephens Hogue, a spiritual direction colleague and educator, gave me absolutely essential critical feedback to assist me in the later stage. Sophie Weeks provided me with important questions and comments, editing suggestions, goodwill, and good solid coaching in the final stage of manuscript revision. All Souls Episcopal Parish in Berkeley, California, gave me the opportunity to present key elements of this work as a Lenten series. My spiritual director and my spiritual directors' peer-supervision group listened faithfully with me as I discerned my path. Dirk deVries and the rest of the Church Publishing crew has been patient and wonderful. My wife, Ruth Meyers, is my dear partner in discernment on so many things. Thank you all so very much.

Introduction

I will lead the blind
    by a road they do not know,
by paths they have not known
    I will guide them.
I will turn the darkness before them into light,
    the rough places into level ground.
These are the things I will do,
    and I will not forsake them.

Isaiah 42:16[1]

When the soul wants to experience something she throws
out an image in front of her and then steps into it.[2]

—Meister Eckhart,
thirteenth-century mystical theologian

SOON AFTER I finished work on my book *Where Two or Three Are Gathered: Spiritual Direction for Small Groups* and was awaiting its publication, I had a series of dreams that I named "The Beasties Trilogy." The final dream of the series went this way:

Mansion and Guard Dogs (March 20, 2012)

I am walking on a paved footpath and come up to a large entranceway to a mansion. The heavy wooden door is carved with scrollwork, and it is open. I have the feeling that I am supposed to go inside. Although I don't recollect many particular elements of the mansion, I do see that it is well-appointed and has dark wood walls. I know that the mansion contains many wonderful collections of rich treasures. There are two large, strong Dobermans inside the house that slowly approach the vestibule as I come to the

> threshold. I feel some caution about the dogs, yet they are not threatening. I pause and sit near the entranceway, considering what I should do and that I should wait until I am in the right state of mind before I enter. The guard dogs casually lie down near the entrance, watching me and awaiting my move.

This dream felt like it had something important to tell me, and I shared it with Ruth (my wife), my spiritual director, my spiritual direction colleague group, members of a small online dreamwork group, and with people I was training to lead small groups in our parish church. Their comments and questions helped me further to explore many of the possible meanings residing in the dream.

Some things became clear to me. I had completed a major life project in the publication of the book on small group leadership and now needed to pause and await clarity about what was next for me. There were several potential projects in which I had some energy and passion, but I wanted time to pray and to consider what seemed best and what might be God's desire for my work.

One person asked me about the dogs, their qualities, and how those qualities related to me. I imagined Dobermans as powerful and loyal guardians in the service of their human master. But I also thought of Dobermans as being potentially violent and vicious. While renouncing the use of violence, I do believe in establishing healthy boundaries. I, too, wish to have my life and work dedicated to the service of my Master, the One to whom I belong. And as a Christian and a priest of the church, I want to dedicate my labors in the service of the God I have come to know through Jesus Christ. Like a Benedictine oblate, I want to act according to the motto *Ut in omnibus glorificetur Deus*, "That God may be glorified in all things."

So I needed to consider my next step carefully, deliberately, and prayerfully, seeking God's wisdom and direction—in other words, I was being called to a time of spiritual discernment. When I was ready, I would cross the threshold into the vestibule of the mansion, that liminal space where I would be leaving the past behind and be shaped anew.[3]

I made a lot of positive associations with the dream mansion that opened for me to enter when I felt ready. I thought of the great sixteenth-century Carmelite mystic Teresa of Ávila and her book *The Interior Castle* (or *Mansions*). God dwells in the final, most interior mansion. That made sense to me. I do not own the dream mansion . . . or at least not alone; it belongs to God, as does the life and the future that I call mine. I also recalled the Gospel passage about the many mansions, or dwelling places, in the Father's house that Jesus goes to prepare for us (John 14).

Time has now passed since I received that dream and first began reflection on its symbols and its possible meanings. As I walked down a country road in England during my sabbatical writing time—this was in the fall of 2013, when I was working on the initial draft of this book—I thought once again of that dream with its mansion, the dogs, and the open door awaiting my entrance. Now I have befriended the powerful energy of the Dobermans, for we, the guard dogs and myself as the dreamer, all loyally seek to serve the same Master of the mansion. I now have crossed the threshold and entered this great place with its rich storehouse of spiritual treasures, and in this book I share with you what I have seen and known from a lifetime as a Christian trying to be faithful to Jesus's call to follow him, and also as a spiritual director and guide over some thirty years. I share examples from my own life as well as professional observation and instruction.

I have always been a dreamer. As a child, I frequently dreamt I was a young African lion, part of a majestic pride lounging by a tree on the savanna. My maternal grandparents' name—Lyon—linked to my childhood. Of course, in the dream, I appeared as a lion, and of course I was part of a pride, for I was very proud of my family. I belonged, and our family was powerful. My grandpa Lyon, an ordained minister in the Disciples of Christ (Christian Church), was well-respected in the Battle Creek, Michigan, community. I benefitted from that relationship in my young life in the church he pastored and in the broader community of which we were both members.

But some of my childhood dreams were dark and anxious. When my parents struggled through the emotionally wrenching process leading to separation and divorce, I remember dreaming that a pack of wolves attacked my father and drove him away from me. I felt terrified that we were being torn apart by vicious wolves. I grieved the loss of his presence. As an innocent little boy, those dreams about the lion pride and pack of wolves told me profound emotional and spiritual truths that I could only apprehend in the form of pictures, symbols emerging from deep within my unconscious through a mysterious source of wisdom.

Both these dreams' symbols expressed felt truths. The pride of lions spoke to me of the power and comfort I felt in belonging to a family, the gift of strong connections in a network of relationships. The pack of wolves attacking my father spoke of the terror and bewilderment I experienced as a young child when marital conflicts led to the tearing apart of a family and to grief from the physical separation of one parent from the home.

Also as a child, I engaged dream symbols with a particular form of conscious play. Sometimes when a frightening dream image threatened to overpower me, I would waken and hold the intention to bring a helper into my dream. As a little boy, help came in the form of the cartoon superhero Mighty Mouse, who I saw in comic books and on television, a children's version of Superman—with cape, super-strength, and the ability to fly. I would replay the dream and encounter the frightening image, then call upon my dream hero to help me. Mighty Mouse would fly into the dream, singing his cartoon theme "Here I come to save the day!" and then fight on my behalf against the threatening dream villain. Often at the end of the revised dream, there would be a sign proclaiming "The End" as in a film.

How has your capacity to imagine and dream changed since your childhood?

What has aided, or impeded, your ability to engage imagination?

All of us, children and adults alike, begin with this capability to engage creatively, playfully, and consciously with the powerful symbols that come to us from our depths; this ability lasts until we sufficiently internalize the dominant culture's rationalistic teaching to ignore dreams, because "they are *only* dreams." And although I am not particularly proficient at the art of lucid dreaming—in which I become aware that I am in a dream and stay in the dream while consciously engaging the images in that dream or choosing to switch to some other scenario—I have had some dreams (lucid or otherwise vivid) that profoundly shaped my spiritual life. I share some of these dreams in this book.

In my early thirties, I first learned about the spiritual power of imagination and meditation. My local Episcopal church sent me to a Christian-education conference led by the great Roman Catholic spiritual formation educator and storyteller Megan McKenna. Near the end of the conference, Megan led us in a guided-imagery meditation, a first for me. Several unexpected symbols emerged in my meditation. Megan suggested imagining Jesus coming to meet us, and the person who came to me, bearing a huge smile, was a cousin of mine. I was puzzled by Jesus's appearing as my cousin, not only because I wasn't prepared for Jesus coming to me as someone I knew in my life, but also because this cousin had a particularly cautious, skeptical outlook on religion. While glad to see him, I wondered why I had unconsciously associated him with Jesus. I pondered that association after the meditation. Finally it dawned on me. This particular relative and I had been close all our lives, even though we lived far apart. In our childhoods we wrote to each other and always looked forward to getting together for an all-too-brief time over school breaks in the summer or perhaps at Christmas. I had no doubt at all that he loved me, as I loved him, unconditionally. It was that unconditional love that my cousin offered me that taught me in this meditation something very important about Jesus and God's love.

The other image that puzzled me came at the end of the meditation. Megan invited us to imagine that Jesus, who had shifted in image to a more conventional form as the bearded young man in a robe, had a gift for us and to receive whatever gift was ours. Jesus gave me a small glass vial of some clear liquid. I asked him what it was. He told me that the vial contained the tears of the world. Again perplexed by this unexpected symbol, I pondered what he wanted me to do with it. Was I to drink it? That didn't seem right. Then I brought the vial close to my chest; it seemed to disappear into my heart. Absorbing those tears of the world given to me in that meditation by Jesus in my young adulthood continues to inform and shape my spiritual life after more than thirty-five years.

In this book I explore the role that symbols, often emerging from our unconscious depths, play in guiding us in our spiritual life and discerning what direction or path God would have us take in our personal, family, and communal lives. Over the years, seeking to follow the desire of the Divine in my own life and family, and as a Christian priest and spiritual director guiding others, I have noticed that there is little written in the spiritual direction literature that focuses on the role of guiding symbols in spiritual discernment.

I contend that the Holy One wants to speak to us, and often does so in the language of powerful symbols arising from the depths of our individual and collective being. The symbols that emerge from our particular life situations that are also deeply connected with our spiritual tradition provide light on our spiritual journey. This light illuminates our situation and reveals God's desire for us personally and in our common life together. This book helps us pay closer attention to those lively, guiding symbols that emerge from the deep source of wisdom and creativity within and around us.

> I contend that the Holy One wants to speak to us, and often does so in the language of powerful symbols arising from the depths of our individual and collective being.

Together we explore a practical model of spiritual discernment and discuss how engaging receptive tools such as contemplative[4] spiritual practices, exploring dream symbols, and participating in sacramental rituals all provide powerful guiding symbols that contribute to the discernment process. We look at varying contexts for discernment, from personal situations to global issues. Questions for personal and group reflection appear as sidebars throughout the book, along with additional examples of guided imagery meditations and further discussion on dreamwork.

I do not intend that my own preference for working with dreams, active imagination, and imagery-based meditation diminish other avenues for cultivating guiding symbols. My preferences reflect my own hardwiring of abilities. You may find that other practices work more fruitfully for you. I encourage you to explore a wide range of practices and claim those that help you in your own unique relationship to God and that fit your own particular set of abilities and interests. Also, feel free to skip over sections of the book if you want to hone in on particular subjects first. The first half of chapter 1 (the general discussion on symbols) and chapter 2 provide the foundation for much of this book. If you want to focus on meditation practices and dreamwork you can go to the sections "Practices Using Imagination" and "The Royal Road" in chapter 3. Then in chapter 4 browse the examples of dreams in the "Personal Direction" section and within "Meditations and Imagination Exercises" in the "Church or Organization" section. And finally, go to the appended section "Additional Guided Meditations and Dream Notes" at the end of the book.

I draw many examples from personal experience. Please indulge me in this more confessional form of personal narrative. I hope that my theology shaped by lived experience brings greater depth to the book. I also share situations in which I served as a spiritual companion for others and witnessed God's grace at work in a variety of contexts ranging from the individual to the communal (marriages/partnerships, families, churches, and organizations).

I also hope that a wide adult audience finds this book a helpful support for their individual spiritual lives, apart from the formal setting of spiritual direction. As in my previous book, *Where Two or Three Are Gathered*, I speak from the particular perspective of a Christian priest and educator; I draw upon that tradition as my primary frame of reference. However, we live in a time of sharing among religious traditions, a mutually enriching process. As a spiritual director—and someone who teaches in spiritual direction training programs—I am in holy conversation with wonderful people from other spiritual orientations and faiths, along with those not rooted in a particular tradition who nonetheless journey with deep spiritual interest and curiosity. I hope such companions find sufficient commonality and benefit in these pages.

I do not write from a disinterested professional perspective with little emotional energy. Rather, based on my own spiritual experience and the companion experiences with others, I deeply believe that God cares about our lives, is passionately in love with us, and wants to guide us.

I intend to help you see how God provides guiding symbols that can be gleaned from your own dreams and spiritual practices. These symbols invite you to draw close to the Holy One. They illuminate your spiritual journey (personal and communal) in creative partnership with the Holy Mystery, the Mystery that desires a deeper relationship with us all.

1

Symbols and Their Kin

Signs, Symbols, Sacraments, and Stories

IF YOU DRIVE a motor vehicle and come upon a traffic light, you must know what those colored lights mean and respond accordingly. Green means go; yellow means proceed with caution and be prepared to stop if necessary; and red means stop. Those traffic signals are signs with one specialized meaning. The meaning is direct and exclusive as far as the laws concerning operating a motor vehicle are concerned. To go against the meaning, especially of the red signal, breaks the law and risks legal consequences as well as places those in the vehicle—and any other person or vehicle at the intersection—in danger. A sign stands for a single thing. A stop sign means the approaching vehicle must come to a full stop. However, there are times when a sign is not just a sign. When an image shows up in a dream or a meditation, it may be a *symbol*.

Symbols differ from signs. Symbols offer multiple layers of possible meaning. For example, I occasionally dream that I work as an orderly in a hospital. An orderly provides personal care to patients, takes vital life signs, and transports patients to various locations for medical treatment. The appearance of the symbol "orderly" might have something to do with assisting those in medical need, being a link to their well-being. The dream says something about that part of me that wants to help or is concerned about a physical problem (someone else's or my own).

I have some personal history of working as an orderly in a general hospital in my early twenties, so being an orderly in my dream might touch upon my young adulthood when I was beginning to make a living in the world. Because I spent two years employed in hospital jobs (including as an orderly), performing alternative service as a conscientious objector during the Vietnam War, there might be a layer of meaning connected to what I consider to be a religious, moral, and sociopolitical issue.

Of course, the wordplay on *orderly* may point to a feeling that things are somewhat out of balance or seem chaotic and that a part of me wants to get my life in order. That particular interpretation often rings true for me. Sometimes I even laugh with recognition when I awaken from an "orderly dream."

On a religious level, I might be seeking the Divine as an agent of care and healing in the midst of the pain and suffering of the world or the chaos of the universe. I want God to bring healing from suffering, order out of chaos. Perhaps an "orderly" archetype—of someone who brings order—exists in various ways in different cultures. I'm sure that you can come up with additional meanings for the symbol "orderly" based on your own frame of reference and personal history.

Symbols are multifaceted images, words, sounds, or actions with many potential meanings that can range from the physical and personal, to interpersonal, social, political, national, archetypal, religious/spiritual, global, and even cosmic perspectives.

> Symbols are multifaceted images, words, sounds, or actions with many potential meanings that can range from the physical and personal, to interpersonal, social, political, national, archetypal, religious/spiritual, global, and even cosmic perspectives.

Where signs have a sense of social consensus about them so that a sign has one meaning, symbols may be interpreted in many ways without consensus that one meaning is the only right or authorized interpretation.

Archetypal psychologist James Hillman writes about going beyond interpretation in the interaction with powerful symbols (he calls them "images"):

> There is an invisible connection within any image that is its soul. If, as Jung says, "image is psyche," then why not go on to

say, "images are souls," and our job is to meet them on that soul level. I have spoken of this elsewhere as befriending, and elsewhere again I have spoken of images as animals. Now I am carrying these feelings further to show operationally how we can meet the soul in the image and understand it. We can actively imagine it through word play which is also a way of talking with the image and letting it talk. We watch its behavior—how the image behaves within itself. And we watch its ecology—how it interconnects, by analogies, in the fields of my life. This is indeed different than interpretation. No friend or animal wants to be interpreted, even though it may cry for understanding. We might even call the unfathomable depth in the image, love, or at least say we cannot get to the soul of the image without love for the image.[1]

The Cross

Certainly in the Christian faith, the cross of Christ provides the most universally recognized symbol. While sometimes bare and plain, at other times the cross appears with flourishes, such as in the design of a Celtic cross. Sometimes the cross includes the figure of the risen Christ clothed in priestly vestments or crowned and adorned in royal majesty. Sometimes it bears the crucified body of Christ. Innumerable poems, hymns, meditations, and theological treatises focus on the cross. The symbol of the cross offers a source of profound devotion, inspiration, humility, compassion, forgiveness, and mystery. For some people, however, the cross can be the cause of painful confusion or outright abuse. A long and terrible history of Jewish persecution and anti-Semitism due to falsely or ignorantly condemning a whole people as "Christ killers" provides one example of such abuse.

In my spiritual direction practice, I sometimes sit with people as they struggle to find an adequate personal understanding of the meaning of the cross and Jesus's suffering and death. Various atonement theories have been offered over the span of Christian history, but none of them seems to fully comprehend the meaning of the cross. The "satisfaction" or "substitutionary atonement" theory developed by Anselm in the eleventh century is particularly subject to criticism for the way it portrays God the Father as demanding a sacrifice that is sufficient to redeem humans from their sinfulness. In this theory, God sends Jesus the Son of God as the sacrifice that satisfies that demand. Many people in our era may find such an image of "father" repellent or even monstrous, although it might not have been viewed that way in earlier centuries.

Other atonement theories emphasize other possible meanings. Jesus's faithfulness to God and finding the right way to live even in the face of the threat of death can be seen as the "moral exemplar" for our own struggles in living moral, purposeful, faithful lives that are compassionate and self-giving reflections of a loving God. Or we might view Jesus's crucifixion as his triumph over all the powers of evil, breaking the hold of evil and death over humanity (*Christus Victor*).[2]

"Coming to the cross" can provide a profound devotional practice. For some it is a ritual practice at a special time of penitence, such as the veneration of the cross on Good Friday. Others may use the imagination in prayer with a contrite heart. One of my most powerful experiences as a spiritual director was as a companion for several years to a pastor in an Anabaptist tradition. At the end of each session he asked me if I would accompany him "to the foot of the cross," and then, as I sat with him in humility, he poured out his heart and soul before Jesus there on the cross of his imagination. It was one of the most beautiful and moving spiritual practices I have participated in.

Language and imagery about the nature of God are highly symbolic and metaphoric. We never fully capture God in conceptual terms; the Divine will always be beyond the language we use. However, symbolic terms help us understand the role of God in our lives and in human history. Many Christians use the symbolic language of the Trinity. Father, Son, and Holy Spirit point to the communal nature of God and how God acts and reveals aspects of God's self in human history and the cosmos. This language runs the danger of becoming encrusted and rigid over time, or of being experienced as an oppressive tool of patriarchy if the understanding of God becomes limited to male gendered attributes. "Creator, Christ, and Holy Spirit" and other ways of naming the Trinity help us break away from the gender-restricted language in

our perception of God. Many other metaphors expand upon our understanding of God—often drawn from poetic images in Holy Scripture—and show up in prayer, theology, and liturgy. Metaphors of *rock,
mother hen, protective eagle, judge, healer, living water, good shepherd*, and
Wisdom are just a few symbols used to expand our images of the Divine
and describe aspects of our relationship to God. What language and
symbols we use about God reflect the way we relate to the Divine and
affects whether we wish to turn to God for discernment. This is crucial,
because if I am relating to a judgmental and potentially wrathful God,
I may not want to seek "God's will" for me. I probably just want to hide
and keep out of God's sight for fear that I will provoke disappointment
and anger. If my metaphoric language for the Divine expresses a positive and loving relationship, I am much more likely to seek what God
desires for me.

Sacraments

The Book of Common Prayer describes
sacraments as "outward and visible signs of
inward and spiritual grace, given by Christ
as sure and certain means by which we receive that grace." So a sacrament is a special kind of sign, a ritual activity with an
external, visible action that we see and in
which we participate, but that also carries
multiple symbolic meanings. A sacrament,
then, is an effective representation of—and
a vehicle for—God's favor (grace) acting
upon us. Many Christian worship traditions recognize two sacraments that were
commanded by Jesus in Scripture: holy baptism and holy Eucharist (Mass, communion
of the Lord's Supper). Some branches of the
Christian church recognize and celebrate
additional sacramental rites: holy matri-
mony, reconciliation of a penitent (confes-

What has been your
own experience
of rituals and
symbols? Do you
recall any situations
when a ritual or
symbol powerfully
affected you? If so,
what occurred?

Have you had any
experience of baptism
or Eucharist or other
sacramental rite that
produced a profound
change in you? If you
are not Christian,
what religious or
spiritual rituals are
important for you?

sion and absolution), holy unction (healing), confirmation, and ordi-
nation. Any ritual provides a process for change. Religious rites focus
on intentionally bringing people into the presence of the Divine with
prayer and holy symbols, and we are affected by that encounter. Sacraments use powerful symbols embedded in divinely graced transformative rituals, intended to move people from one state of grace to another.
For example, with holy baptism, in which a person is ritually sprinkled
or fully immersed in water, grace is conveyed that has multiple powerful and transformative meanings:

- the purifying effect of the ritual washing away of sin
- the participation in Christ's death and resurrection, dying to
  an old self and taking on the new self in Christ
- the initiation of the newly baptized into the body of Christ the
  church, sometimes with a new name
- the receiving of the Holy Spirit and being marked as Christ's
  own forever, sometimes signified by applying chrism.

In truth, the reservoir of symbolic meaning in these primary sacraments of baptism and holy Eucharist runs so deep that we may never
be able to fully comprehend the vastness of God's love for us shown in
these unitive rites. There will always be something more that the rites
can tell us about divine love, just as there is always something more to
the holy mystery we call God.

Stories

Within the sacraments, stories provide powerful symbolic images and
actions that convey various meanings and interpretations. The sacrament of holy Eucharist, for example, contains a retelling of the story
of Jesus's last supper with his disciples and his command for them to
receive the bread as his body and the wine as his blood whenever they
gather in remembrance. This sacred story is often cast within a broader
narrative of the history of God's saving actions drawn from Jewish
scripture as well as Christian Gospels and Epistles.

In many Christian liturgical traditions, *remembrance* is not just of something that happened once upon a time, it also actively links the past sacred story with our present situation, with Christ present with us now in our ritual participation in the breaking of the bread.[3] Bread and wine become powerful sacramental symbols of Christ's Presence, and in eating the sanctified bread and drinking the holy wine there is a level of interpretation in which we are renewed as the holy people of God and become Christ-bearers in the world.

Other sources of stories and symbols prove useful as we reflect upon meaning, wisdom, and direction. Dreams contain stories—or fragments of stories—that include symbols that become objects of interpretation, adding additional levels of possible meaning. Guided-imagery meditation provides a story that elicits symbols and actions. Reading Scripture may entail imaginatively engaging sacred stories. And I (as well as you) bring my own unique story, my life narrative.

When I go to see my spiritual director, I often tell stories about what is going on in my life—situations that challenge, fascinate, or frustrate, stories that feel like a special gift to me, bore me, or that call forth some other feeling or desire. Often I try to understand these parts of my story more deeply. We look together at the narratives and the symbols within the stories, exploring their possible meanings and the spiritual invitations and directions God may have for me in my unfolding life.

> What happened to you recently that seemed sacred or holy in some way? What does this say about the presence of the Divine in your life?

I provide this discussion about signs, symbols, sacraments, and stories to help us understand the power symbols offer. Symbols give rise to thought and feeling. They elicit reflection on meaning and interpretations on multiple levels. In this book we explore how symbols emerge and guide us in deepening our spiritual lives and in discerning our most authentic direction amid the multiple forces that call for our attention and the choices and possibilities on our life journey. Symbols that deeply connect us with our spiritual tradition and our own particular life circumstances provide a light on the path.

Guiding Symbols and Divine Communication

Wisdom lies deep within us. Its source is the Holy One who resides within the core of our being as the indwelling Presence. We are each a tabernacle for the Presence, though we are frequently dulled to this incredible gift through our attachments, the tugs of our little sins, our ignorance, and our self-absorption. And yet, from our depths, the Divine beckons us through the language of symbols to attend to its guidance, as this Presence desires that which is truly best for us and for our fullest participation in the unfolding unity, destiny, and joyful fulfillment of all things in God.

In the Christian faith, we speak of God the Holy Spirit who dwells within us as our advocate, counselor, and guide, and who gives us gifts that we exercise for the benefit of all. We remember in the final chapters of the Gospel of John Jesus's assurance to his disciples that he brings them into the abiding unity of the Father with the Son, and that the Holy Spirit will come to lead them into fuller truth (see John 14–17). The second chapter of the Acts of the Apostles tells the story of the coming of the Holy Spirit upon 120 men and women gathered in an upper room in Jerusalem on the day of Pentecost. Peter grounds this experience of the coming of the Spirit in the foretelling of the prophet Joel:

> In the last days it will be, God declares,
> that I will pour out my Spirit upon all flesh,
>   and your sons and your daughters shall prophesy,
> and your young men shall see visions,
>   and your old men shall dream dreams.
> Even upon my slaves, both men and women,
>   in those days I will pour out my Spirit;
>   and they shall prophesy.
>
> Acts 2:17–18; Joel 2:28–32

The Jewish tradition of the nearness of God, the knowledge of God, and the presence of the Holy Spirit is not restricted to the anticipation of the prophet Joel. For example, the eleventh chapter of the book of Numbers tells the story of Moses, who is being overwhelmed by the burden of leadership. God tells Moses to gather seventy elders. Moses gathers the seventy elders and places them around the "tent of meeting," whereupon the Lord takes some of the spirit that was on Moses and transfers it to the seventy elders, who then prophesy. The story continues: two elders, Eldad and Medad, who missed the event at the tent of meeting, also receive the spirit and prophesy. A young man sees what happens to Eldad and Medad and reports this to Moses. Joshua, Moses's lieutenant, calls for Moses to stop them. Moses replies, "Are you jealous for my sake? Would that all the Lord's people were prophets, and that the Lord would put his spirit upon them!" (Num. 11:29).[4]

The poet of Psalm 139 speaks of the intimacy of God's spirit and the inescapability from the presence of God. The whole psalm offers a magnificent meditation, but one portion of it in particular vividly conveys the sense of the immediacy of the Presence within:

> Where can I go from your spirit?
>> Or where can I flee from your presence?
> If I ascend to heaven, you are there.
>> If I make my bed in Sheol you are there.
> If I take the wings of the morning
>> and settle at the farthest limits of the sea,
> even there your hand shall lead me,
>> and your right hand shall hold me fast.
>
>> Psalm 139:7–10

Divine wisdom and guidance is available, but often it requires the arduous work of making a journey. Sometimes the journey requires physical travel, but always it requires some interior exploration. We can assume the writer of Psalm 139 made an interior wisdom journey to discover the ubiquity of God's presence and intimacy.

But sometimes the sacred story of a physical journey also stands as an archetypal symbol for the interior wisdom journey. We find one such interpretation of the journey of the wise men (or Magi) in Matthew 2. In this story, the wise men from the East observe and follow a star to seek the newborn king of the Jews. As they ask about this new king

What do you understand from your own spiritual tradition about how the Divine attempts to communicate with you?

in Jerusalem, the reigning King Herod feels threatened and asks his counselors where the child might be. Herod deceptively asks the wise men to share information with him on where they find the child so he also can honor him. The wise men continue to follow the star to a house in Bethlehem where they give homage and gold, frankincense, and myrrh to the child of Mary. Then, warned in a dream of Herod's murderous intention against the child, they leave by a different route.

On a literal level we can approach this situation, as the wise men did, as a warning that Herod is lying and intends to murder this new king. That interpretation should not be discounted, for certainly clear and direct warnings can come to us through dreams. It was realistic to question the sincerity of Herod given the potential threat a new king would pose to his power. Other rulers, then and now, have used deceit and violence to suppress or prevent possible loss of power. Our commemoration of Holy Innocents' Day during the Christmas season remembers this grim story. Herod commands the slaughter of all children under two years old in the vicinity of Bethlehem after learning that the wise men had taken a different route back after visiting the holy child. Fortunately, according to this narrative, an angel warns Joseph in a dream about Herod's intention, and the holy family flees to Egypt after the wise men's visit and before the slaughter begins.

We can also interpret this story as an interior journey of wisdom. We seek enlightenment (following a star) and look for the royal child that has been born within us. The light guides us on the path to the Divine. The inner journey is done with others who honor true wisdom and the traditions that bear divine grace for humanity, so we are not alone. As each of us encounters the inner divine royal Presence, we offer that which represents our true self. It is a costly offering but also a joyous one. In the journey we also must consciously recognize the jealous and fearful parts of ourselves, those parts separated from our deepest desire that, if unrecognized, could harm and supplant the vulnerable innocence and purity of the divine mystery that could dwell at the center of our lives. Dreams might warn us of those shadowed parts of ourselves that need to be acknowledged and reconciled or otherwise dealt with before they cause severe damage to our well-being.

Both the Hebrew and Christian scriptures contain many stories in which a dream symbol or an image from meditation provides divine revelation or a guiding message to a person, a community, or a nation. Consider, for example, the role dreams and their interpretation take in the saga of Joseph from the time of his conflict with his brothers and being sold into slavery to his rise to power as the chief administrator of Pharaoh's storehouses. Those tales are rich in dreams and interpretations that are instrumental in developing the plot in Genesis 37–41. Earlier stories of the patriarchs also present powerful, revelatory accounts of dreams or visions. In Genesis 15, Abram—later renamed *Abraham*, with the new name itself symbolic of a changed identity and new life— encounters God in a vision and receives a promise of greatness and offspring. Abram responds with belief in the promise and makes a sacrifice to God. In what seems like a dream state, he sees the covenant ratified by God, who passes through the sacrificed creatures as a smoking fire pot and flaming torch.

Jacob, afraid of his brother Esau's wrath after Jacob tricks his father Isaac into receiving Esau's birthright and blessing, leaves his family in Beer-sheba and travels toward Paddan-aram in search of a wife. On the journey, he sets up camp at one wilderness place, takes one of the stones there for a pillow, and goes to sleep. Then he has a dream that could be considered the greatest archetypal dream of the Hebrew Scriptures:

> And he dreamed that there was a ladder set up on the earth, the top of it reaching to heaven; and the angels of God were ascending and descending on it. And the Lord stood beside him and said, "I am the Lord, the God of Abraham your father and the God of Isaac; the land on which you lie I will give to you and to your offspring; and your offspring shall be like the dust of the earth, and you shall spread abroad to the west and to the east and to the north and to the south; and

all the families of the earth shall be blessed in you and in your offspring. Know that I am with you and will keep you wherever you go, and will bring you back to this land; for I will not leave you until I have done what I have promised you." Then Jacob woke from his sleep and said, "Surely the Lord is in this place—and I did not know it!" And he was afraid, and said, "How awesome is this place! This is none other than the house of God, and this is the gate of heaven."

Genesis 28:12–17

In this dream, we share with Jacob a vision of correspondence between the divine life and our earthly lives. God is not far off and uninterested in human affairs. The gate of heaven can be as close as where we are.

There is a wonderful story of Jacob wrestling with the angel of God as his brother Esau catches up with him years later. Their pending meeting could bring about disaster or reconciliation. As Jacob anticipates meeting his brother the next day, he spends the night in a wrestling match with a "man" (his shadow? conscience? God?). Jacob refuses to let the man go until he receives a blessing, so the wrestling partner strikes Jacob's hip and puts it out of joint. The man then asks Jacob for his name and says, "You shall no longer be called Jacob, but Israel, for you have striven with God and with humans, and have prevailed" (Gen. 32:28b). When Jacob asks for the man's name, he refuses to give it, but instead gives Jacob (now named Israel) his blessing. Beware: when we struggle with important things in life with our conscience intact and ask for divine wisdom to discern the right way forward, we may find ourselves wrestling with God. The struggle might well give us three gifts:

▸ a limp, meaning that struggles can be costly and we will be thrown out of our self-centeredness;
▸ a new name, meaning that we will gain some new sense of identity;
▸ a blessing, meaning that some creative outcome will emerge.

An exhaustive treatment of the dreams and visions in Holy Scripture is beyond the scope of this book.[5] Suffice it to say that both the Old and New Testaments present many dreams and visions as vehicles for God's guidance, both personal and collective. I now consider how these kinds of revelations did not end with Holy Scripture.

> **Which of the Bible examples spoke most powerfully to you? Can you say why? Are there other examples in scripture that are important to you?**

I am going to look briefly at three historical developments that have particular impact on engaging symbols as a guide for spiritual direction in our lives:

- ▸ first, the "showings" or visions of Julian of Norwich;
- ▸ second, the contribution of Ignatius of Loyola to spiritual direction;
- ▸ third, the development of depth psychology and its application to spiritual understanding.

Julian of Norwich: *Revelations of Divine Love*

Lady Julian (ca. 1342–ca. 1413) was one of the great fourteenth-century English mystical theologians. As a young woman she prayed for three graces: first, to be consistently mindful of Christ's Passion; second, to experience sickness severe enough to bring her near death at age thirty; and third, to receive three wounds. She sought the wounds of true contrition, loving compassion, and a deep longing for God. Shortly after she turned thirty, Julian experienced a severe illness and received the last rites of the church. She remained gravely ill. Then, on a Sunday, the pain left her and she received fifteen visions (showings) related to God's love for humanity and the cosmos, centered on the cross of Christ. The next day she received a sixteenth vision.

These visions convinced Julian to become an anchoress, living her life enclosed in a church and dedicated to Christ, serving as a spiritual guide to many people who sought her out—including the mystic Margery Kempe, who dictated what may have been the first autobiography in the English language. Julian spent twenty years in theological reflection on those visions and wrote both a shorter and longer version of her visions and contemplation of their meaning. Julian is credited as the first woman to write a book in the English language. Her reflections display a remarkable depth of theological understanding on the love of God and the compassionate nature of Jesus Christ. She refers to the motherhood of God and of Jesus, and her work has profoundly influenced Christian mystical theology and spirituality.

Reading Julian's *Revelations of Divine Love* for the first time when I was a seminarian was a truly spiritually formative experience. Drawing on still earlier theologians such as Anselm, Julian's portrayal of God and Jesus as "mother" spoke of the tender and compassionate nature of the Divine. Jesus, in his sacramental self-offering, nurtured humanity by his body and blood. I read this at a time when there were vigorous debates in The Episcopal Church about expanding the use of metaphors for God and including feminine imagery. The movement for the expanded use of images for the Divine was not only supported by a multitude of scriptural metaphors for God, but I learned through Julian of Norwich that it was also supported by centuries of theological writing and prayer.

I persistently struggle in my life to accept my limitations as a servant of God and Christ. I get anxious about whether I have done enough and judge myself as falling miserably short of being the "good and faithful servant." Reflections that Julian wrote about the revelation concerning the lord-and-servant parable provide a wonderful healing balm to my soul.[6] In that revelation a servant first stands face to face with his lord. They behold each other in great love. The servant receives a mission from his lord. Excited about the opportunity to serve the lord that he loves, the servant eagerly sets off to fulfill the mission. No sooner does he begin the journey than he falls into a ravine. He is so injured and caught in mire that he is unable to get out or even move his head to see anything. The servant is filled with shame and remorse at his inability and failure to serve the lord that he loves so dearly.

In the meantime, the lord, who has a different perspective on the situation, looks at the servant with great love and respect. The lord sees the servant's desire to be good and loyal to his master and his willingness to offer service and suffering. The lord will restore and richly reward the servant. God then leads Julian to understand that the servant is Adam and therefore is the archetypal representative of the human condition, as is the restored Adam through Christ's suffering and faithfulness. God sees our love and desire to serve, and judges us with the divine love and compassion which we cannot provide for ourselves from our limited human perspective.

Lady Julian's contribution to mystical theology stands monumental. But also she is representative of many remarkable visionary women and men in history who dared pray for insight and deep revelations from God, as well as leading others into their own relationship with the Holy One. Some, like Lady Julian, left a record of their encounters with the Divine. Among many spiritual writers and mystics are Mechthild of Magdeburg, Hildegard of Bingen, and Teresa of Ávila, as well as John of the Cross. These visionaries support us in our own desire to know God more deeply and to open ourselves to divine guidance and wisdom for ourselves and our world.

> Are you familiar with the writings of any of the Christian mystical theologians? Other religious traditions also have their great historical spiritual teachers. If you are aware of some of those women and men, what is it that deeply connects with your own spiritual life and desires?

Ignatius of Loyola and the *Spiritual Exercises*

There are many treasures in the history of Christian spirituality, but for our purposes one development in the sixteenth century made immeasurable contributions to contemporary spiritual direction by showing ways of engaging Scripture imaginatively, using guided imaginative forms of meditation, and attending to the affective dimension of our spiritual lives in relationship to God. Ignatius of Loyola (1491–1556) desired to be a glorious soldier, but in a battle at age thirty, when he was defending a castle in Pamplona against a French attack, he sustained severe wounds from a cannonball. One leg was injured and the other

Read a passage of Scripture such as a Gospel story. Close your eyes and, using your imagination, enter into the scene. Are you one of the characters mentioned in the scene or an observer? What do you notice and feel as the story progresses? What thoughts and questions come to your mind? If you wish, ask people questions, engage in a conversation, or initiate your own actions within the scene. When finished with the meditation, journal about it or debrief with others. Did insights emerge about a situation or direction you are considering in your life?

Three additional meditations are

broken. He was taken to his castle in Loyola, Spain, to recover from the injuries. His broken leg needed to be set (without anesthesia), but it did not heal. The leg needed to be rebroken and reset. Ignatius's condition worsened, and he was told to prepare for death. Surprisingly, he recovered, though when his leg healed, a portion of bone protruded below his knee, and that leg was shorter than the other. The doctors sawed off the protruding bone, and Ignatius tried stretching exercises, which failed to level his legs. He walked with a limp for the rest of his life.

During Ignatius's convalescence, depressed that he had to give up his dream of being a soldier, he underwent a gradual process of spiritual conversion while reading books on the life of Christ and on the lives of the saints. He reoriented his life's dream from becoming a great soldier in the military to becoming a soldier for Jesus Christ. He practiced various spiritual exercises to help deepen his life in Christ and compiled some of these exercises to assist other spiritual directors in leading retreatants. Later, in mutual discernment with his companions, the Society of Jesus (Jesuits) was formed.

Ignatius's *Spiritual Exercises*, which he revised and expanded throughout his life, reflects his desire for deepened commitment to Christ and discernment of the vocational path that Christ calls forth. Ignatius designed the *Spiritual Exercises* for a four-

week directed retreat making use of scripture, imagination, affect, and meditation.[7]
Thematic weeks, variable times, and a gradual movement from head to heart and from
meditation to contemplation mark the design of the *Exercises*.[8] He wrote the *Spiritual
Exercises* as a guide for spiritual directors,
based on what Ignatius had found helpful in
his own conversion process, using the spiritual practices available to him. The spiritual
director adapts the exercises to the individual retreatant's needs. A person might use
all their time on just one "week" or focus on
the prefatory "Principle and Foundation."

One of the hallmarks of the *Spiritual
Exercises* is the invitation to use our imagination in meditations. Some spiritual exercises ask us to enter with our imagination

mentioned related
to making a decision:
providing advice to a
stranger who is facing
a similar situation,
imagining you are at
the point of death,
and standing before
the judgment seat of
God. If you are facing
a major decision or
seeking direction is
there one or more
of these meditations
you could use?

into particular scenes in the Gospels, listening to and taking the role
of different characters, noticing how this affects us. For example, the
second contemplation of week two instructs the retreatant to enter a
prayerful time of imaginative meditation on the Nativity of Jesus. This
contemplation (meditation) begins with a prayer for God's grace to
know Jesus more intimately, love him more intensely, and follow him
more closely. The retreatant imagines the scene at the birth of Jesus
and notices all its characters, what they say, how they feel, and how
they respond to God. The fuller context of the hardship the holy family experienced and the purpose of Jesus's birth and death on the cross
for the retreatant should be recognized.[9] The retreatant also reflects on
how the exercise affects him or her.

While some imaginative settings are based on Scripture, such as the
nativity scene we just considered, others are opportunities for imagining situations not directly drawn from Scripture but that nonetheless
help us as we deliberate. For example, in week two of the *Spiritual Exercises* is a section about making an "election," or discernment, around

a choice and wishing to follow God's call. Here one of the suggestions about making a good decision invites us to imagine that a person we have never met comes asking for advice in a similar matter. How would we advise that person? Or another suggestion is to imagine you are at the point of death and have the freedom and clarity of that moment. What decision would you make? Or a third meditation is to imagine that you are at the final judgment and standing before Christ, reviewing your life with him. What decision would you have wanted to make about this choice?[10] The Ignatian meditation on Scripture, imagining life situations to bring us closer to God, continues as an important resource for discernment.

Ignatius's counsel on the movements of the affective spiritual states of consolation (toward God) and desolation (away from God) provide further value for spiritual guidance. For example, at times of spiritual consolation, God feels most present to us, we experience comfort and peace, and we make better decisions. We then ask ourselves if the path we are considering will bring us even nearer to God. We should also recognize that this felt experience of nearness and grace will pass. And so in the time of spiritual consolation we store up a well of memories of what it is like to receive God's graces.

But, Ignatius counsels, when in a state of spiritual *desolation*, we feel more distance between ourselves and God, and we should *avoid* making decisions. We will tend over time to oscillate between these affective states of consolation and desolation. So we should wait out the times when we experience desolation, persevering in our faith and trusting in God's love for us even if we do not feel the closeness. During desolation we draw from our memory—like drawing from a well—what it was like to receive the graces of consolation, and remind ourselves that those times again will come to us.[11]

How does Ignatius's discussion of spiritual desolation and consolation fit with your understanding of the movements in your own spiritual life?

With Lady Julian's "showings" as profound examples of symbols for contemplating our relationship to God, and with Ignatius of Loyola's meditation exercises and teachings on consolation and desolation, we see how symbols serve as important guides illuminating our path. Other visionary saints and spiritual teachers in Christian history add their own rich symbols and ways of prayer, although I cannot give them the attention they deserve.[12] However, that doesn't need to stop you from learning from them on your own.

Depth Psychology and Re-appropriating the Power of Symbols

The Christian liturgical tradition in the West developed and led people over many centuries into the power of the sacraments. Christian mystical writers and theologians endowed the church with a wealth of reflection and understanding about spiritual life. Tragically, due to the twin forces of the Protestant Reformation's suspicions of religious superstition and the Western enlightenment's emphasis on rationalism, we lost much of the appreciation for the inner guidance and wisdom of symbols arising from dreams and meditational practices.[13]

However, there was a rediscovery of the value of symbols in the developing field of depth psychology in the nineteenth and twentieth centuries. Sigmund Freud (1856–1939) made pioneering contributions to understanding the relationship between the unconscious and conscious aspects of the psyche and in therapeutic work with manifest and latent meanings of dream symbols in psychoanalysis. His younger colleague Carl Gustav Jung (1875–1961) branched off on his own in the development of analytical psychology and in archetypal theory. Jung found it important to bring not only dreams but also cross-cultural symbols, myths, and religion into his understanding of psychology. Jung's expanded study and recognition of the importance of religious meaning for analytical psychology had profound implications for prayer, meditation, and dreamwork practices as sources of deep inner wisdom and divine guidance.[14]

What is your own understanding of the interplay between psychology and spirituality?

In 1968 two Episcopal priests, John Sanford and Morton Kelsey, brought the contributions of Jungian psychology into direct con-

If you decide to use the meditation on death and rebirth from Dr. Simonton, are there any safeguards you should consider? For example, are you asking someone who has a reasonable knowledge of meditation and safety to lead you? If you are dealing with any significant mental health issue that could weaken your boundaries, I encourage you to think about and talk about the movements in the meditation with a trusted companion during the exercise, rather than immersing yourself in the scenes though imaginative visualization.

versation with mainline Christian spirituality. Sanford, a Jungian psychoanalyst as well as an ordained minister and the son of Agnes Sanford, a major leader in the inner-healing movement in mainline Christianity, published *Dreams: God's Forgotten Language.* Sanford argued for bringing Jungian archetypal understandings to bear on the interpretation of meaning in dreams, including dreams presented in Scripture. His book *The Kingdom Within: The Inner Meaning of Jesus' Sayings* (1970) continued to focus on the inner meaning of Scripture through a Jungian perspective.

Kelsey, a parish priest and scholar who taught at Notre Dame and studied at the Jung Institute in Zurich, Switzerland, also contributed breakthrough understandings of the power of symbols to illuminate our inner world and provide revelatory insight. He published *Dreams: The Dark Speech of the Spirit* in 1968 and in 1974 revised and released the book as *God, Dreams, and Revelation.*[15] Here Kelsey provides comprehensive historical scholarship coupled with dream theory and dreamwork practice in a thorough treatment of Jewish and Christian experience of dreams. One of many books he wrote on the lively interface between psychology and Christian spirituality, *The Other Side of Silence* presents Christian meditation, dreamwork, and practices using imagination and art.[16] I am personally deeply indebted to Morton Kelsey's writings on dreamwork and meditation and other creative methods for exploring the inner world and encountering God within; through his writing I discovered a vital Christian path for my own spiritual journey.

While a seminary student in the early 1980s, I spent my first summer taking a clinical pastoral education course as part of the pastoral-care staff at a general hospital. As a student chaplain I covered both a general medical-surgical floor and the major burn unit. I began researching what spiritual and psychological resources could help patients. In my study I came across the work of Dr. Carl Simonton, a radiologist and oncologist, who used mental imagery to help manage pain, fight disease, and improve quality of life. He published *Getting Well Again* in 1978, which continues to support many in looking at the mind-body connection to wellness.

One of the imagery meditations he offered his patients was about death and rebirth. This is my adaptation of Simonton's meditation to introduce guided-imagery meditation. It presents powerful themes of discernment:

Meditation on Death and Rebirth

In this meditation, visualize as best you are able the different scenes presented and explore the feelings, thoughts, and conversations associated with them.

1. Imagine the situation that is to bring on your death.
   - What are the circumstances surrounding your impending death? Accident? Illness?
   - How do you feel? To whom do you talk?
   - What do you say or do?
2. See yourself moving toward death, experiencing the dying process, and seeing who is present at your place of death.
   - What is said and felt?
3. Attend your own funeral. Who is present? What is said and felt?
4. See yourself at the moment of your death.
   - What occurs?
   - What happens to your consciousness?

5. Your consciousness goes out to the Source of the universe. Imagine yourself in the presence of God.
- ▸ What is happening?
- ▸ How do you feel?
- ▸ What do you and God do?

6. Review your life in detail in the presence of God.
- ▸ What pleases you about your life?
- ▸ What would you have done differently?
- ▸ Do you have resentments?
- ▸ Is there any significant unfinished business?
- ▸ Are you at peace in all of your significant relationships?

7. You come back to Earth. You have a new body and can create a new plan for your life.
- ▸ Would you choose the same parents or new ones?
- ▸ How about brothers or sisters? Friends?
- ▸ What would your life's work be?
- ▸ What is essential to accomplish in your new life?
- ▸ What is important in your new life?

8. Recognize and appreciate that the process of death and new life is continuous in your present lifetime, every time you change your beliefs and feelings.
- ▸ What would you like to take with you from this meditation to aid you in creating the next phase of your life?

9. Return from your meditation and reflect on the important insights you have gained.

The meditation emphasizes that life is a constant process of death and rebirth, and you have opportunities to initiate changes while still alive.[17] I have used a form of this meditation many times for individuals and groups, sometimes resulting in profound insights.

Before I began leading others through this meditation, I asked my clinical pastoral education supervisor to lead me. I discovered with complete surprise that the overwhelming love I received from the Presence and those nearby this Being was so great that I didn't want to come out of the meditation. Years later I still remember the powerful feeling of that unconditional, absolute love freely given to me. My perspective shifted and was reframed in the anticipation of my own death.

Since the late 1960s and 1970s, other resources have come out that relate to our subject. Carolyn Stahl Bohler's book *Opening to God: Guided Imagery Meditation on Scripture* was released in 1977 and revised and expanded in 1996. The early edition offered my first opportunity to read about guided imagery based on Scripture and to use it in individual or group settings. I found it remarkable that an ordained United Methodist minister at that time was crediting Ignatius of Loyola for having used Scripture-imagery meditation centuries before. Bohler's book opened my eyes to the depth of this Christian practice in church history.

In 1982, Dominican Sister Marlene Halpin published *Imagine That! Using Phantasy in Spiritual Direction,* the first contemporary book I have seen intended for spiritual directors leading guided-imagery meditations. Elizabeth-Anne Stewart (Vanek) published *Image Guidance: A Tool for Spiritual Direction* in 1992, a work that also addressed the importance of attending to the symbols that arise for spiritual directees. Robert A. Johnson's *Inner Work: Using Dreams and Active Imagination for Personal Growth* (1986) introduced students of spiritual direction to the use of dreams and archetypal symbols that arise from active imagination in order to help directees explore their inner wisdom, needs, and desires for wholeness.

In recent years a number of books have been written on the subject of spiritual discernment. Two come from recognized leaders in practical theology and spirituality, both of which address spiritual discernment for individuals and couples: Elizabeth Leibert's book *The Way of Discernment: Spiritual Practices for Decision Making* (2008) provides useful information on practices and exercises for discernment in personal decision-making. Dwight Judy offers very helpful guidance on listening within and attending to external practical issues during major life transitions in *Discerning Life Transitions: Listening Together in Spiritual Direction* (2010). I mention several other books when I explore spiritual discernment for a church or other organizational context in chapter 4.

The late 1970s and early 1980s brought remarkable growth in the development of spiritual formation centers for training lay and ordained spiritual directors through certificate or degree programs; this growth continues. Many of these centers offer training programs for an ecumenical or interfaith population. Because of these centers, we have many people now skilled and available to guide individuals or groups through spiritual direction or retreats.[18]

In this chapter we began our exploration of the functions of symbols and their kin, especially clusters of symbols arising from sacramental rites, dreams, and meditations. We looked at some of the powerful visions and dreams in Holy Scripture. We noted that the importance of symbols as sources of revelation and wisdom diminished with the rise of the academy, Protestantism's attempt to eradicate superstition, and the rationalism of the enlightenment era. Yet Lady Julian of Norwich, Ignatian spirituality in the sixteenth century, and the rise of depth psychology in the nineteenth and twentieth centuries strongly attested to the value of symbols as sources for insight and wisdom. Since the late 1960s, the guiding potential of symbols as God's language speaking to us from our personal and collective unconscious has gained increasing recognition.

2 Spiritual Guidance and Discernment

Contemporary Spiritual Direction and Guidance

SOME OF YOU practice as spiritual directors. Some of you meet with a director. I also write for those *not* involved in formal spiritual direction. In chapter 1, I discussed Ignatius of Loyola and his influence on spiritual direction as well as his contribution in recognizing the way that imaginative meditation on Gospel stories or other situations assists in discernment. I have described what goes on when I visit my spiritual director and mentioned that dreamwork and active imagination are often part of the training for aspiring directors. This is to say that a spiritual director, spiritual companion, or guide (there are various names for this ministry) is a good resource person if you wish to explore spiritual and holistic meanings of symbols that emerge in your life and how that might lead you to holy wisdom. That person is not likely to tell you what the symbol means for you, but instead she or he will help you uncover various possible meanings; *you* decide what rings true most deeply for you.

In *Where Two or Three Are Gathered: Spiritual Direction for Small Groups,* I describe various "spiritual companionship" groups that churches, institutions, and spiritual directors typically offer. A facilitator, perhaps a lay leader, trained in small group leadership and dynamics, leads these groups. These groups offer mutual guidance, community, and spiritual support. Some of these groups are short-term, meeting four to ten times. Some offer chances to renew membership for additional terms. Other groups may be ongoing and run for years. A group might focus on dreamwork, or guided-imagery meditations, or meditating and reflecting on Scripture, or practicing a group form of spiritual direction for a designated member, or other ways of helping support members in their spiritual lives. Membership in such a group helps tremendously in discerning what God desires for us in our lives.

Of course, good spiritual guides and companions exist beyond those formally trained for that particular ministry. Our friends, pastors, therapists, colleagues, life partners, family members, or wise people of faith—found in our churches, synagogues, and other settings—may serve as spiritual friends, helping us notice the movement and invitation of God in our lives. Public figures, living or dead, or historic saints may also serve as exemplars, helping inform our lives and encouraging us as we walk on our spiritual path. The Holy Spirit actively ministers to us through any number of people, including those we encounter "by chance" for a brief time.

> If you belong to a Christian church, do you think the meditation on the resurrection appearance of Christ would be of interest to the church's leaders and members?

Sometimes a spiritual director or other consultant will help a couple, family, church community, or other organization reflect on their present situation and the steps toward discerning their direction and vocation. For example, I was invited to serve as consultant to St. Clement's Episcopal Church in Harvey, Illinois, during a major transition in the congregation's life.

Comes from Above, Found Within

In a training session for a parish discernment team, I led a guided-imagery exercise imagining Christ appearing at a meeting of St. Clement's Church leaders. The meditation went like this:

Resurrection Appearance to the Disciples[1]
(patterned from John 20:19–22
or Luke 24:36b–40, 44–49)

In this meditation, allow frequent pauses for people to visualize or "think through" different scenes. Ask the group to focus par-

*ticularly on how Christ might engage us as a Christian commu-
nity rather than as individuals.*

1. Imagine that your congregation or church leaders
gather to try to decide an important question. *What is that
question?*

2. Imagine the resurrected Christ appearing in the midst
of the gathering.

- What does the Christ look like?
- How do you feel about Christ's presence?
- What about others in your church? Does anyone say
  or do anything in response to Christ appearing?

3. Are there things that your church community fears or
worries about? Is there something they seek direction for that
needs to be brought to Christ? What does Christ say or do
about your fears, concerns, or request for direction?

4. Christ offers you peace. What is that like for you and
the rest of the community?

5. Christ empowers your community to a mission beyond
itself.

- What might that be?
- What does it feel like to receive the power of the
  Spirit?
- What gifts or abilities seem to emerge for your com-
  munity's empowerment?
- Are you aware of resistance or confusion or other
  barriers to receiving this empowerment? If so, you
  can ask Christ for guidance.

You might ask the Christ for a word or phrase or gift that
speaks to the nature of your community at this time.

Receive whatever Christ has to give you on behalf of your
community.

Ask whatever additional questions necessary to understand this word, phrase, or gift.

> The time has come for you to say goodbye and return
> from the meditation with your memories of this encounter.
> Make your goodbyes in any way that feels appropriate.

Following the guided-imagery meditation, I asked each person to describe what happened. One member imagined the leader of the parish food pantry as the spirit of Christ at a vestry meeting. The topic the vestry discussed was the need for a mission statement. Phrases she heard associated worship, nourishment, and nourishing others. Then she offered a tentative statement, "We gather to receive nourishment so that we may in turn nourish others."

How did you find yourself reacting to the story of the parishioners in their meditations? Have you had anything similar happen to you in a meditation?

In another's meditation, the caring and nourishing feminine dimension of Christ was present. The words "stay and serve" stuck with her. Christ's spirit allayed people's fears of diminished energy and admonished the group, "You can meet together anywhere—but if you meet here, you serve."

In the junior warden's meditation, everyone on the vestry worried about little concerns. Christ pulled up a chair and said, "Don't sweat the small stuff—concentrate on what you know you need to do." Someone asked, "What about the diocese?" "I'll take care of the diocese!" replied Christ.

In the senior warden's meditation, Jesus came as a soft, loving light, like a flowing chiffon scarf. The feminine image surprised her. The people had many questions about the liturgy and the search process for a rector. The Presence looked at them, but left it up to the people to determine the answer. She still felt lack of clarity, but it wasn't so distressing now. She didn't want to return from the meditation.

For another member of the discernment group, the imagined meeting was filled with doubt, "What are we going to do?" Everyone wanted to give an opinion. The Presence was like a mediator; the meditator said in his imagined meeting, "He's not answering the question. You already know what to do." He felt the church had a call to reach out to the community. "We have a service to offer—but there's fear of stepping out."

"It was an annual meeting type of setting and the question was, 'What do we do now?'" reported the other member of the group. Jesus appeared to the gathering as overwhelming purple light. Then, replacing the light, everyday-looking people came and sat next to the parishioners. They talked about drug problems and about the need for a rector in a way that comforted "our people." There was a sense of peace, like a burden lifted, and a little child held the group member's hand. The Light spoke out that they would be empowered to do even more. There was doubt, but the light got brighter. Words she associated with the meditation were: "Our growth in faithfulness means growth for the church."

> What are your thoughts about the parishioner's comments that the "answer" comes from above but is found within us?

Following this debriefing, I invited the group members to sit silently in prayer for about fifteen minutes with a question for discernment related to the parish. When the silence ended, a member shared this discovery: *The answer to our questions comes from above but needs to be found within ourselves.* Her disclosure is a fair description of spiritual discernment work within a community. In spiritual discernment we seek God's guidance in a matter of importance and so there is very much a sense that the answers or directions have an origin beyond us—a gift of grace that "comes from above." But spiritual discernment also requires a profound inner work of prayerfulness that evokes the guidance of primary symbols which connect the discerning community to the great themes of Christian faith, such as God's providential care and love, mission, healing, and reconciliation—so the "answer" or direction is found "within ourselves."[2]

As you can see, the guided-imagery meditation evoked strong encounters with Jesus in all the participants' inner worlds. I had worked with these people in a number of prior training sessions, so they already were developing their capacity to listen imaginatively and prayerfully

Spiritual discernment is seeking to discover the deepest, truest direction for a person or community in accord with the creative urging of the Spirit.

The words "discern" and "discernment" are used in various contexts, including in business and religious settings. What do you see as distinctive about "spiritual" discernment? How is it similar to other forms of decision-making?

prior to this particular exercise. They strived to become a discernment team that assisted the vestry and the congregation in shaping a new vision and mission statement for the church, and that helped lead the process of calling a new priest. I will say more about them and their discoveries later on. But for now, let's explore how the process of spiritual discernment and listening for God's wisdom in the decisions and directions we face in life does, indeed, come from *above*—but is found *within*.

The Spiritual Discernment Cycle

Christians have practiced spiritual discernment since the earliest centuries. Paul mentions discernment in 1 Corinthians 12:4–11 as a spiritual gift alongside the gifts of wisdom and knowledge. The Bible offers ample stories of individuals, families, seers and prophets, kings, and others seeking to discern the right direction, the direction that God would have them take. Christian monastic writers John Cassian (fourth century) and John Climacus (seventh century) write about the importance of spiritual discernment. And already we have briefly discussed some of Ignatius of Loyola's counsel and practices for discernment.

Francis de Sales (1567–1622), a Roman Catholic bishop of Geneva and spiritual director, viewed Christian life as a courageous dance of discernment between the vastness of God's will and the concrete situations that we enter into with faith. "Let us live courageously between the one will of God and the other."[3] Francis proposed two "wills" of God. One he calls the "signified will of God," the vast will of the Divine that permeates the cosmos, so vast that we humans cannot fully comprehend it. It is the big picture of God's will for humanity and for our place in the great scheme of things. Although vast and beyond us, we do have resources that help us comprehend God's signified will. We have Holy Scriptures, the teaching and guidance of the church, the ability to pray and meditate, and our felt sense of God's will for us.

Francis also spoke of a second will, the "will of God's good pleasure." This second will of God operates with providential care for us in the concrete and particular circumstances of our lives. Opportunities and situations open up and close down for us like doors. We come up against both limitations and unexpected, new possibilities. In our particular situations, sometimes what we perceive as God's signified will for us gets thwarted or waylaid. In those situations, we are invited to live into the mystery of God's providential care and hidden guidance that constitute the will of God's good pleasure. God is not like a puppet master in these situations, but God's care and guidance is at work with us in and through the specific situations. Our task is to live with courage and faith between these two perceived wills of God. Francis de Sales offers us a good foundational understanding of living a dynamic, alert, and responsive life in relationship with God, sensitive to the particular situations that affect the life choices we make.

What, then, do we mean by spiritual discernment? "Spiritual discernment" means to disclose, uncover, or discriminate among the forces underlying an issue or choice of directions and to seek as much clarity as possible as to what path or direction God would have for the individual or community.[4] To put it even more succinctly: *Spiritual discernment seeks to discover the deepest, truest direction for a person or community in accord with the creative urging of the Spirit.*

In entering into spiritual discernment we make bold assumptions:

- ▸ God desires a creative and dynamic relationship with us as individuals as well as with our families, communities, and societies in this time as much as in the past.
- ▸ God offers guidance for our personal and our community's most authentic development if we are willing to listen. The Christian spiritual tradition variously describes God's guid-

The Spiritual Discernment Cycle

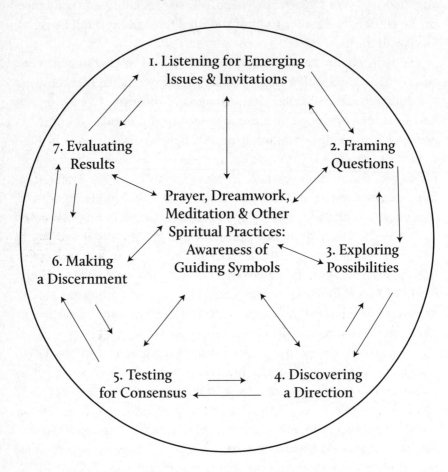

1. Listening for Emerging Issues & Invitations

7. Evaluating Results

2. Framing Questions

Prayer, Dreamwork, Meditation & Other Spiritual Practices: Awareness of Guiding Symbols

6. Making a Discernment

3. Exploring Possibilities

5. Testing for Consensus

4. Discovering a Direction

ance as the "will of God" or God's desire, direction, calling, or vocation.

▸ Individuals and communities can learn how to discover more sensitively God's direction for them.

▸ The church has, as part of its tradition, tools of spiritual discernment to apply to our contemporary needs for personal and communal spiritual direction and decision making.

▸ God often communicates through a combination of receptive and imaginative forms of prayer, formational use of Scripture, and primary symbols through such sources as dreams and active imagination.

There are various ways of describing the movements of spiritual discernment. Here we look at a model of the steps in spiritual discernment that emphasizes the importance of prayer and other practices that open us to guiding symbols.

A Dance with the Divine

The Jesuit spiritual guide and writer Fr. Thomas Green once remarked, "God is the lead dancer and the soul is the partner completely attuned to the rhythm and patterns set by the partner. She does not lead, but neither does she hang limp like a sack of potatoes."[5] I confess to being a reluctant social dancer. I have to muster up a bit of courage and put aside my self-consciousness to join in social dancing. So I know that to engage in the dance requires the ability to step out and enter in trust, sensitivity, and responsiveness to my dance partner. I feel and hear the music in my partner's movements; I "let go" into my body. If I overcome my own inner reluctance, take the risk, trust, and release, I actually do have fun with my partner. Whether we think of ourselves dancing with God who takes the lead (Thomas Green) or dancing courageously between the two wills of God (Francis de Sales), we have a pretty apt metaphor for spiritual discernment.

So think of the movements of spiritual discernment as dancing with the Divine. As you see from the diagram, the steps are not always a linear progression; we may find ourselves moving back and forth between the various steps. In some situations, we may even find that we skip a step. Not only are there changes between steps, but also movement inside and out, between the center, that is, between our spiritual practices that seek God's guidance, and each of the steps.

Reaching discernment—or any step along the way—may uncover new issues or invitations from God for new discernment; so, the cycle begins again. In truth, spiritual discernment is a *lifelong* dance with God, a way of being in relationship with God and with the people and situations in our spiritual journeys. Let's look in some detail at the particular steps and at the center of the spiritual discernment cycle.

1. *Listening for emerging issues and invitations.* Spiritual discernment is a conscious action that requires active listening. We listen with the awareness that, hidden within issues and situations, God may invite our faithful and deliberate response. Concrete situations offer the context for our discovery of God's desires and directions for our life and the lives of our communities. For St. Clement's Church, the emerging issue was calling a new rector after the sudden resignation of a long-term rector, a difficult interim situation, and a failed relationship with the following rector. However, underlying *that* issue were various invitations from God to own their grief and confusion over the losses of the long-term rector and some major lay leaders; to recognize and honor their need for healing; to become free to look at ways they could configure their ministry and common life; and to discover and articulate their deepest sense of who they were and what they were called to be prior to searching for a rector.

In all the major events in our individual and communal lives, God may be inviting us into spiritual discernment. Examples of issues or concerns inviting spiritual discernment include:

- ▸ sorting through new possibilities following—or in anticipation of—a job loss
- ▸ moving into retirement
- ▸ receiving a new job offer
- ▸ making choices of vocation and career
- ▸ deciding whether and how to move a person closer to you or further away from you in social and emotional intimacy
- ▸ deciding if a love relationship is moving toward deeper commitment and possibly marriage
- ▸ making "quality of life" and "end of life" decisions for ourselves or others

- ▸ deciding whether to (and when to) start a family or add new members
- ▸ looking into the possibility of making a major geographic move
- ▸ evaluating how your money and time are spent and what values undergird those decisions.

All such situations seriously affect our lives as individuals, couples, and families.

So too in work, church, organizations, and society, we are called upon to make communal decisions. These events become God's invitation to engage in spiritual discernment. Any such event has underlying issues important to disclose, consider, sort out, and address with wisdom and grace.

2. *Framing questions.* The kind of questions we ask give powerful shape and direction to our inquiry and set limits on the scope of our discovery. In order for spiritual discernment to occur, we need to frame our inquiry and structure our path of discovery in a way that makes the search for God's direction central. So the kind of questions we ask makes a big difference. For example, if a church experiences a crunch in its budget, one might ask, "What expenses can we cut and still maintain the highest quality possible in our church programs?" That question is probably familiar to many vestries, bishop's committees, and clergy.[6] This management-oriented question focuses on a problem with little reliance on imagination. It seeks a technical adjustment in the financial system of the church, one most concerned with minimizing disruption and finding an outcome that maximizes efficiency.

A spiritual discernment–oriented question is of a different order, such as: "How might God want us to handle our budget? What might God wish us to emphasize in our financial stewardship?" The discernment-oriented question takes the governing body down a path of examining its sense of the mission of the parish and how it is funded, as well as looking at the policies and assumptions that shape its understanding of stewardship, faith, and fiscal responsibility, and how they usually go about seeking God's guidance in the structuring of their budget. This kind of question grounds the exploration of the issue in a sense of God's presence in and desire for the community.

We can ask similar questions around our personal or family budget. Perhaps most of the time we are, in fact, just wanting to balance the budget—usually a good thing—but this goal doesn't disclose much about ourselves, our motivations, and our relationship to God. On occasion we might feel prompted to go deeper and look at how we are stewards of resources God has given us, not only for our well-being but also for the benefit of others. What values and priorities does our household spreadsheet and checkbook disclose? What goals do we hold for ourselves?

3. *Exploring possibilities.* This phase of a deliberation should be familiar to anyone who knows creative problem-solving techniques. It begins with a time for entertaining many possibilities, for brainstorming, for being open to creative and new inspiration. Get every possibility out on the table for consideration. Do not evaluate, criticize, or place any limits on how crazy or wild the possibilities are that may emerge from this first effort.

Eventually all the options are out in the open. It then becomes time to narrow the possible directions down to a few that have deeper merit. When the options are narrowed down to two or three, gather all the available data relevant to the value and feasibility of each option, including information from all parties affected by each choice.

At this point, discernment begins to depart from customary problem-solving techniques. Collecting data also means noting what symbols emerge from your inner world and from the external environment that relate to each option, and what feelings emerge from considering each option. Consider following an Ignatian approach, beginning with the following steps:

▸ First, list all of the *disadvantages* if I/we *do* this option.
▸ Second, list all of the *disadvantages* if I/we *don't do* this option.
▸ Third, list all the *advantages* if I/we *do* this option.

▸ Fourth, list all the *advantages* if I/we *don't do* this option.
▸ Repeat for all other options using the same four considerations.

Another Ignatian practice for exploring the options is to take an equal amount of time to live fully into each option as if it were your choice. While living with each option, pay attention to how you feel, the quality of your prayer, Scripture or symbols that come to mind, and the quality of your relationship to God. After living with one option, take an equal amount of time living with the others. When you have lived with each option as if it were your final decision, see if one of those alternatives connects better with your deepest sense of purpose and brings you into a closer relationship with God.

In experiencing the differences among options, Ignatius offers the symbol of a drop of water falling onto either a rock or a sponge. Does it feel as if the option has a harsh quality, like a drop that falls on a stone and splashes? Or does it feel like a drop that falls on a sponge and is peacefully received and absorbed?

Spiritual discernment requires something other than a business model or a decision based simply on preference or inclination. As Christians practicing spiritual discernment, we do so prayerfully, anticipating an inner freedom that seeks God's deepest good rather than only personal satisfaction. We pray that we might have the inner freedom to desire that which God desires for us.

Results of the investigation are shared completely and weighed based on that inner freedom of discernment. Care should be given to noticing whether an option seems to bring the discerners closer to God or draws their attention further away from God to other things.

4. *Discovering a direction.* Eventually we may get clarity and peace around a particular option. Things may seem to converge; one direction has a special sense of rightness, of blessing about it. Sometimes it seems perfectly clear to everyone that this choice is the right one, that God has revealed this direction to us. However, there are other possible results from exploring the options. We may feel stuck in confusion, and

so we might need to see if other options emerge, or sit with the options for longer to see if greater clarity emerges as we continue to gather information and pray. In other situations, we may choose a direction with a sense that one option seems best . . . but we could be wrong. If we reach the place where one of the options seems best, it is wise to check with others, the next step.

5. *Testing for consensus.* In community life, as well as individual life, some things are too important to ram through as a personal preference or with a majority vote where there are "winners and losers." The spiritual discernment traditions emphasize the importance of group unity and cohesion by providing processes that avoid win/lose decision making. Major questions of policy, identity, congregational sense of ministry, and church or organizational mission are best decided through consensus building. Consensus does not necessarily mean unanimity. But it does mean that everyone responsible for the decision has been fully heard and that their perspectives on the multifaceted truth have been received.

> If you are a church leader, how do you see the church community engaged in major issues and decisions?

In seeking consensus it is helpful for the community, before attempting discernment, to establish a policy about what percentage constitutes consensus. For example, the community may decide to require a minimum of three-fourths-majority vote. If the agreed-upon level of consent is not reached, the community will need to deliberate further and probably go back to an earlier step in the discernment cycle.

People may voice serious reservations and still abide by the wisdom of the consensus. If there are strong concerns, enter the reservations in the record of the deliberations. Concerns may prove prophetic, and the decision may need to be revisited with further discernment.

In individual discernment, the idea of testing for consensus is not as formal, but the principle still holds; even as a person seeks the views of community—church members, family, friends, partner, spiritual director—when exploring possibilities (step 3), so it is important to seek input while gathering data . . . and after you have made a tentative decision (step 4). Questions to consider are: Does this direction seem to fit well with others' views of you? If this decision affects others, how is it likely to affect them? And do others agree with your direction, or at least are they willing to go along with it? How many people do you need to hear concerns from before you consider that you may be on a wrong track?

6. *Making a discernment.* Once consensus has been reached, we say that we have "discerned the path to be taken." Hopefully the process has been done both with faith and humility. Usually, once discernment has been made, there is a sense of God's peace, which does not ignore challenges, and you may discover a release of creative energy for living into the direction. However, sometimes there is still uncertainty. That does not necessarily mean we have made a wrong discernment. If a decision must be made, sometimes we just need to pray for the right choice and then decide. We live into the mystery of our human limitations and the mystery of God's purposes. We embrace the humility of recognizing that, in the life of faith, we trust beyond ourselves and our ego's desire for certainty. If we have made a wrong discernment, we will probably recognize it later and begin a new time of discerning, for God does not abandon us. In fact, God is amazingly creative with us.

> In your own experiences of personal and shared decision making and seeking direction what spiritual practices do you regularly use?

7. *Evaluating results.* As we live into the direction we have discerned, note and evaluate the results of the discernment. Is this path, this direction into which we are living, producing good fruit?[7] What emotional and spiritual climate is generated by this direction? Do we see the results we expected or is something else happening? If concerns were expressed by a minority, is a situation emerging that justifies their concerns? Are new issues or invitations emerging from this path that call for a new round of discernment?

Prayer, Meditation, Dreamwork: Awareness of Guiding Symbols

Located in the center of the chart and permeating discernment is the prayerful dimension of living. Discernment includes a contemplative dimension in which receptivity to God's leading is valued and sought. We may move between the receptive silence, radical emptying, and holy mystery of the *apophatic* dimension of prayer, which involves appreciation for negation and the mystery of God, and the images, thoughts, and relational truths of the *kataphatic* dimension of prayer, which incorporates a positive way of knowing, including knowing God.[8] Awareness of words that have power for us, Scripture, images, music and lyrics, dreams, events, sacraments—all potentially are ways that God might whisper to us of divine desire. A prayerful and discerning life cultivates an appreciation for the potential of God, through symbolic language, to guide us.

In a very real sense, spiritual discernment is living in a reverential relationship with God and with your companions. This way of discernment and prayer takes you to questions that touch the deepest parts of you and your world, and is a way of living with those questions with a freedom and trust that is truly graced.[9]

Not every decision requires thorough spiritual discernment, even though we live prayerful and discerning lives. A lot of things are not weighty matters, and we make decisions without much concern about how the decision affects us and those around us. We may experience such a solid feeling about an important decision that there doesn't feel like there is any question about it.

A couple of times my wife was invited to consider seminary positions. She asked for my thoughts. In one situation I strongly felt that the location wouldn't be a right fit for us. On another occasion, we barely considered the position because it was overseas and on a short contract, and, although we discussed feeling some attraction to the novelty and adventure, neither of us could see it as a good possibility for a couple with dual vocations and ministries.

However, in considering other career opportunities for Ruth, it seemed like the timing and the situation could be right for her. I knew that there would be reasonable possibilities for developing or redeveloping my spiritual direction ministry in those settings. In these cases, a discernment process was important, and the results supported our mutual desires to serve in ministry.

Discerning the Symbols

I contend that symbols may emerge from our dreams, meditations, and other sources to provide powerful guides in our lives and in the decisions we make. In the model of the spiritual discernment cycle, the central activity (and way of being) employs prayer and meditation throughout and invites awareness of potential guiding symbols. These emerging symbols themselves may need discernment rather than just being accepted uncritically as having come from God or from our deep self's wisdom. We need to look critically at the symbols and test them for evidence of ego-centeredness, self-defensiveness, the lure of temptation, grasps for certainty or success, and other distractions and distortions from God's wisdom and path.

How do you decide what might be a genuine "revelation" or "insight" when the source comes from beyond our normal capabilities? What do you think is necessary to determine an authentic "guiding symbol" in order to safeguard a healthy (in all ways, including spiritually) sense of direction?

The synoptic Gospels (Matthew, Mark, and Luke) all tell the story of Jesus going into the wilderness for forty days following his baptism and being tempted, or tested, by the devil. Mark does not give any details about the temptations, but Matthew and Luke do. Jesus, in his fasting, has a vision or dream encounter—or multiple encounters—with the devil. Jesus discerns the source of the temptations and his true purpose and path in ministry. After he overcomes this trial in the wilderness, Jesus begins his public ministry. The refining fire of the wilderness temptations helped clarify and strengthen Jesus's self-identity, his understanding of the one to whom he belonged, and his purpose in life (Mark 1:12–13; Matt. 4:1–11; Luke 4:1–13).

The early Christian literature on the desert elders, the *ammas* and *abbas*, from the *Life of Antony* by Athanasius and the collected sayings of the desert fathers and mothers offer many stories of visionary encounters with demons and the need to discern the truth. In doing battle with inner demons, one grew stronger in faith and moved toward the purity of heart that brought a person closer to God. In our discernment of the symbols that come to our awareness, we ask such basic questions as:

- ▸ What is the source of this symbol that holds power for me or for us?[10]
- ▸ Does the symbol seem to be a temptation, or a graced gift related to a divine call?
- ▸ Is the symbol life-giving even while it might be challenging?
- ▸ Does the symbol bring us beyond our selves alone?
- ▸ Does the symbol speak to our deepest sense of truth?
- ▸ Does the symbol seem consistent with our best understanding of God's great desires for humanity as revealed in Scripture and in our spiritual teachings? Does it lead us to engage such themes as healing and wholeness, forgiveness and reconciliation, mercy and compassion, justice and true peace?
- ▸ Does the symbol speak of the paschal mystery,[11] the way of the cross, and new life in Christ?

By exploring such questions we test the symbol for its validity as a guide.

As we venture more deeply into spiritual practices and discernment, we inevitably become aware of and sensitive to encounters with evil. Our rationalistic and empirically centered culture dismisses evil as superstitious nonsense, makes it into entertainment, or tries to reduce it all to a biochemical imbalance and medicate it. Charles Williams, an Inkling companion to C. S. Lewis and J. R. R. Tolkien, wrote gripping and thoughtful Christian novels about encounters with evil in England. Scott Peck, in *People of the Lie,* observes something spiritually deep and malevolent in people he describes as "clinically evil" . . . even though they may be recognized pillars of the community. Morton Kelsey provides solid study and counsel in his book *Discernment: A Study in Ecstasy and Evil.* There are spiritual forces or powers that are willful, intelligent, and that cause personal, social, and global harm. As mysterious as evil might be, evading our attempts at full understanding, we are spiritually naive if we fail to recognize that evil is real and that it impacts our world. In the 1979 Book of Common Prayer these questions are asked of baptismal candidates or of those who are sponsors or godparents of infants and children:[12]

> *Question* Do you renounce Satan and all the spiritual forces of wickedness that rebel against God?
> *Answer* I renounce them.
> *Question* Do you renounce the evil powers of this world which corrupt and destroy the creatures of God?
> *Answer* I renounce them.
> *Question* Do you renounce all sinful desires that draw you from the love of God?
> *Answer* I renounce them.
> *Question* Do you turn to Jesus Christ and accept him as your Savior?
> *Answer* I do.
> *Question* Do you put your whole trust in his grace and love?
> *Answer* I do.

What does the word "evil" mean to you? How do you determine whether something is evil? How do you discern what to do in such a situation? What stories do you have about encountering evil?

What difference, if any, is there between evil and a shadow part of your psyche?

As we study spiritual discernment, recognize that we are not only to attend to symbols of God's presence and direction, but also, inevitably, to symbols of evil and how evil affects us individually and communally.[13]

Be mindful, however, that even negative or seemingly "demonic" symbols may provide wisdom if we are grounded in our faith and values. We learn from those shadow or negative parts of ourselves, recognizing them as warnings of our own destructive potential or of aspects of ourselves in need of forgiveness, healing, and integration into a greater wholeness. Elsie Landstrom beautifully expresses this graced movement toward integration in the poem "Song to My Other Self":[14]

> Over the years I have caught glimpses of you
> in the mirror, wicked:
> in a sudden stridency in my own voice, have
> heard you mock me;
> in the tightening of my muscles felt the pull
> of your anger and the whine
> of your greed twist my countenance; felt your
> indifference blank my face when pity was called for.
> You are there, lurking under every kind act I do,
> ready to defeat me.
> Lately, rather than drop the lid of my shock
> over your intrusion,
> I have looked for you with new eyes
> opened to your tricks, but more,
> opened to your rootedness in life.
> Come, I open my arms to you also, once-dread stranger.
> Come, as a friend I would welcome you to stretch your
>   apartments
> within me from the cramped to comforting side.
> Thus I would disarm you. For I have recently learned,
> learned looking straight into your eyes:
> The holiness of God is everywhere.

A dream that I had soon after I seriously began considering a call to ordained ministry was a big challenge. For about a year before this particular dream, I had experienced a series of lucid dreams. In this type of dream the dreamer is aware of dreaming and exercises some conscious control—or even changes the dream to pursue some predetermined theme. In my determination to seek encounters with the Holy, I had been successful in shifting scenes in lucid dreams to scenes that had a spiritual context. We look at some of those later. But this time was different—in the dream I encountered an unexpected strong evil over which I felt powerless:

Breaking an Old Woman's (Hag's) Neck
(March 28, 1979)

I'm dreaming of doing world-record broad jumps with a friend, show him how I can float through the air, down a sidewalk, and then realize the reason I can float is that this is a dream.

I ask for Christ's presence, but he doesn't come into the dream. There is a wizened woman present, and I tell her that sometimes God and his angels are slowed by Satan's forces, like when Daniel finally met the angel in his vision. I then start testing whether I'm still in a dream by rising to the ceiling several times. Then the old woman, who feels evil to me, asks me to break her neck. It feels like a powerful and irresistible temptation—and then her neck is broken by my thoughts, and she dies while several men shoot her. I start losing clarity. I am confused and confess, to a young policeman in my dream, that I may have used an occult practice and feel devastated by my actions. My parish priest is horrified at the brutality done to the old woman. I'm taken to a courtroom for my trial, but I have no lawyer, although the court tries to get one for me. I go to a window and pray that God's will be done and resign myself to God's care. I sit next to my parish priest and sob, full of remorse. I am filled with shame and guilt at what I have done.

There are many possible interpretations for this dream; I will only reflect on those that speak most deeply to me. At the time I had the dream, I still had a fresh memory of the years I had spent studying Eastern spiritual and esoteric practices, shamanism, and occult literature, dabbling in spiritual practices from those sources along with illegal drug use. I landed in a very dark and disoriented place. At this time, I had a terrifying dream encounter with an overwhelmingly powerful evil being that offered me everything I had previously wanted in my quest for personal power. I had to choose the direction of my life. In that dream I pleaded for Jesus to help me, and that recognition of my need for Christ's help became instrumental in my eventual return, nearly a year later, to the Christian faith. I discuss that dream later.

Since that first terrifying dream I had other dreams that I believed held positive messages and encouraged my spiritual growth. So this dream of killing the hag knocked the wind out of my sails. Perhaps I had become ego-inflated and overconfident at my supposed progress, including at what I thought was my ability to control my dreams for positive outcomes. I now see the evil old woman as an encounter with the "deadly thought" of pride and a warning of the violence it could unleash in me, even unwillingly.[15] I had to recognize that parts of me are not under my conscious control, and powerful forces within and beyond me are perfectly capable of doing evil to others and to my own self. I experienced existential shame like the apostle Paul described, "For I do not do the good I want, but the evil I do not want is what I do" (Rom. 7:19).

Coming as it did near the time that I was beginning to seriously consider exploring ordained ministry, the dream was a major lesson in humility. Even now I am grateful for the dream image of the parish priest who, amidst the horror of what I had done, was willing to sit with me. Perhaps that priest symbolized the person I hoped I might become, but at the moment I only saw the sinful, broken, weak, violent part of me that I thought had been overcome.

Jesus and the Grandmother
Another example of the need to discern a symbol occurred in a spiritual direction session with a seminarian on the path to ordained ministry, who was concurrently doing academic doctoral studies. He recognized the lack of support he felt from his family, especially a grandmother, about this choice of careers. He believed he was disappointing them because he hadn't gone into a high-status, high-paid profession. His grandmother preferred he stop this nonsense and get a "real job." I suggested that we take this conflict into a visualizing prayer and have

Jesus mediate between him and his grandmother. He agreed to try this meditation.

I set up the scene: he and his grandmother are in a church or other sacred place; Jesus is there, too, standing between them. He is to tell Jesus his concern, and then his grandmother is to share her views. Jesus will then freely talk to both of them. There was silence while my directee engaged in the meditation. He then opened his eyes to signal he was finished . . . and reported that *Jesus had taken his grandmother's side!*

We were both flummoxed by this outcome. How could Jesus have disregarded this directee's call to ministry and have told him that his grandmother was right, that he should get a "real" job? Amidst our laughter and bewilderment it was clear that this "Jesus" of the meditation needed to be more fully discerned. We have, from time to time, come back to that symbol. While my directee did indeed need a "real" job, as in part-time work to help pay expenses while in graduate studies, it didn't seem coherent with other discernment feedback that he should quit the path of ordained ministry. Quitting seemed more a temptation than a direction, which required looking into the forces that seemed to affect the meditation.

I do think, and I believe my direction client also does, that the internalized images of Jesus and the grandmother represent how the strong forces of our cultural materialism—and it is a very real tension that many clergy also feel as that profession shifts more and more to the edges of social respect and seeming relevancy. Those now in seminary, moving toward holy orders or academic teaching degrees related to religion, are well aware of this social shift to a post-Christendom era alongside the long and steady decline of mainline church populations. Professional ministry is a high-risk vocation in our time, and many are well advised to have a second set of skills available for making a living. And yet the need for financial security—and the anxiety generated from a less certain income-producing vocational choice—can become a major barrier to discernment. Dare we trust that God's providential care will also suffice? Matthew 6:25–34 provided the anchor for this spiritual direction client, challenging the anxiety over whether he would have his material needs met. In this passage Jesus admonishes his followers to "strive first for the kingdom of God and his righteousness, and all these things will be given to you as well."

Earthquake

One of the saddest situations I know of concerning a failure to properly discern a powerful symbol occurred in the neighborhood where my parents lived when I was a seminarian. A neighbor suddenly died; his widow and the extended family were understandably bereaved. The widow began using automatic writing to attempt to communicate with her dead husband, and messages started coming to her warning of an impending, massive earthquake. Deeply concerned for her safety, the safety of her loved ones, and the well-being of the city, she spent a large amount of money to reinforce her home and amass goods in preparation for the coming devastation. The family sent warnings to the city to prepare for the earthquake. But there was no earthquake—not externally. She and her family suffered a violent shaking of the foundation of their lives; they experienced a massive loss in the death of a loved one, then projected that loss onto their community. An earthquake had indeed come, but the true need was for grief support and not earthquake-proofing her house.

Refrigerators

When I was consulting for St. Clement's Church as part of its parish-wide training in discernment, I began by leading people in an awareness exercise inspired from exercises I had found (and used personally) in Anthony de Mello's *Sadhana, a Way to God*.[16] In this "Listening for God" exercise, I led the group into and out of sustained silence using a meditation chime. During the silence I invited them to notice any external sounds and asked them to wonder, as the sounds came and went, whether the sounds might be voices of God's presence in and through creation. I then asked them to focus on listening within themselves, again with the possibility that the listening might take them to a sense of God's presence.

During the meditation, one of several brand new industrial-sized refrigerators in the back of the parish undercroft was running rather noisily. When I invited people to share some of their experiences of the meditation, the leader of the food pantry, a major parish ministry, had been deeply moved; she explained that the refrigerator motor brought her an awareness of God's work in their mission of feeding hungry people. Another parishioner, who was on the vestry and a former member of the Chicago Trade Authority, heard the refrigerator noise as God saying they needed to fix it because it was running too much and costing too much. Of course, both were right.[17]

"Francis, Go and Repair My House"

In 1204, Francis of Assisi experienced an auditory vision that marked the direction of his life. His friend and companion, Bonaventure, describes this event:

> One day when Francis went out to meditate in the fields he was passing by the church of San Damiano, which was threatening to collapse because of extreme age. Inspired by the Spirit, he went inside to pray.
>
> Kneeling before an image of the Crucified, he was filled with great fervor and consolation as he prayed. While his tear-filled eyes were gazing at the Lord's cross, he heard with his bodily ears a voice coming from the cross, telling him three times: "Francis, *go and repair my house which, as you see, is falling into ruin.*"
>
> Trembling with fear, Francis was amazed at the sound of this astonishing voice, since he was alone in the church; and as he received in his heart the power of the divine words, he fell into a state of ecstasy. Returning finally to his senses, he prepared to put his whole heart into obeying the command he had received. He began zealously to repair the church materially, although the principle intention of the words referred to that Church which Christ purchased with his own blood, as the Holy Spirit afterward made him realize . . .[18]

We need to look critically at the symbols that come to our consciousness as we seek a deeper relationship to God and attempt to discern our path in life and in the choices and decisions that come our way. Symbols have layers of possible meaning; we filter them through our personal and collective life experience and faith tradition. Although great wisdom emerges from our dreams, meditations, prayers, and other practices, it is critical to recognize that the symbols and the meaning evoked often need to be carefully discerned *within* the fuller process of spiritual discernment.

Via Negativa

> My Lord God, I have no idea where I am going. I do not see the
> road ahead of me. I cannot know for certain where it will end.
> Nor do I really know myself, and the fact that I think that I am
> following your will does not mean that I am actually doing so. But
> I believe that the desire to please you does in fact please you. And
> I hope I have that desire in all that I am doing. I hope that I will
> never do anything apart from that desire. And I know that if I do
> this you will lead me by the right road though I may know nothing
> about it. Therefore will I trust you always though I may seem to
> be lost and in the shadow of death. I will not fear, for you are ever
> with me, and you will never leave me to face my perils alone.[19]
>
> —Thomas Merton

This prayer by Thomas Merton brings us into the heart of the apophatic prayer experience and the not-knowing that may be part of our attempts to discern God's desire for us. We do not always know our way, and sometimes we are even confronted with the mystery of ourselves. In those times the best we are able to do is offer our unknowing and the mystery of our life to the care of the Divine One. The negative way is a difficult and trackless path, but sometimes that is the journey we must take. It, too, brings us wisdom and may eventually point us to a direction. Most important, the negative way provides us the opportunity to develop a faithful relationship with God beyond certainties and securities. In this section I explore the role of apophatic spiritual experience in discernment.

Life Is a River?

The old rebbe was nearing death. His disciples gathered at his home to accompany him through this end time and to hear his last words, which, as the tradition would expect, would summarize his life's experience. The followers of this great Jewish teacher overflowed his home. His inner core of disciples gathered around the rabbi in his bedroom, with his number-one disciple standing next to his bed with paper and pen in hand. "Father," said the number-one disciple, "you have been with us so long and we have benefited so greatly from your years of experience and deep wisdom. Now we await with you the fulfillment of your time on earth, and you're passing over to our ancestors in Abraham's bosom. Before you go we want to know, father, what is life?"

> What have you been taught about the *via negativa* (apophatic) dimension of spiritual life though your church or other faith context?

The beloved master slowly gathered his strength, got up on one elbow, and then the other, looked into his disciple's face and replied: "Life? What is life? Life, my son, is a river!" And with that pronouncement, he fell exhausted back onto his pillow.

Throughout the room the phrase was repeated by one disciple to another, "Life is a river!" The message flowed out into the hallway and spread through the entire house. "Life is a river!" Out to those gathered on the lawn and into the street it flowed: "Life is a river!" Until someone on the edge of the street said, "What? Life is a river? What does that mean? It seems kind of dumb to me."

Then, back from one to another came the questions. "What does that mean? How can life be a river? We don't understand."

Finally the questions flowed back into the bedroom and to the number-one disciple, who had the responsibility of explaining everything once the rebbe died. "Wait, father! Don't go yet! We don't understand! How is life a river?" cried the disciple.

Ever so slowly, by the grace of the Almighty One, the old sage slowly collected his remaining strength. He got up on one elbow, then the other, looked his beloved disciple in the face, and said: "So, maybe it's not a river."[20]

The story illustrates something important about symbols: they both *reveal* and *hide* meaning. This story invites us to peer into the nature of reality and to experience its mystery. Life is, indeed, a river . . . and maybe it is not. It is in coming upon the mystery that defies rational and neat explanations that we will explore now.

In the traditional landscape of Christian spirituality there are two major arenas of encounter with the Divine. One way is the affirmative way, the *via positiva.* This positive way is also called kataphatic, or world-affirming, spirituality. In this part of the landscape, various spiritual paths use practices that help reveal God. The *via positiva* posits that God is knowable through nature, Scripture study, imagery meditation, active prayer practice, theological constructions, music, and other sources.

Another way of encounter is negative, the *via negativa.* This negative way is also called apophatic, or world-denying, spirituality. It is a spirituality of not knowing, of stripping away, of letting go, of being with the mystery of the holy Presence that is God beyond the names and images. The *via negativa* invites us to explore the silence, the darkness, the emptiness, the loss, the poverty of spirit, the need to change direction. It leads us to the hidden Presence barely hoped for when we find ourselves "wandering in the wilderness" and far from knowing how to get to our "promised land." It takes us to the wisdom of the broken heart, the longing for that which cannot be contained, and the mystery that is so close that it cannot be objectified and seen and so is felt as absent. It is the spirituality of the "dark night" of the senses and soul and spirit that sixteenth-century Spanish Carmelite mystical theologian John of the Cross writes about in prose and poetry. It is a development in the stages of prayer described by his elder Carmelite companion and spiritual director, Teresa of Ávila. It is the contemplative prayer of the *Cloud of Unknowing* by the anonymous fourteenth-century English spiritual director.

In spiritual desolation following the loss of my first marriage, I struggled with the ability to pray in the way I had before my married life shattered. Up until then, prayer and imaginative meditation had come easily. With the loss of the marriage, I felt as if my life had collapsed; spiritual desolation and emotional depression took their toll in my inability to concentrate. The words of set prayers often felt meaningless. I decided that I would simply offer one psalm daily as my best effort at prayer—as my attempt to stay connected to God. In that grim time certain psalms or fragments of psalms began to speak deeply, like Psalm 27:14: "Though my father and my mother forsake me, the Lord will sustain me" gave me some solace. I found myself clinging to life-giving words from Psalm 30:6: "Weeping may spend the night, but joy comes in the morning." However, mostly I felt the deep depression of Psalm 88:19: "My friend and my neighbor you have put away from me, and darkness is my only companion." Later, when I was struggling to rebuild my vocational ministry, the words that often came to me were from Psalm 31:12b: "I am as useless as a broken pot."[21]

In those periods I needed to do the hard inner work of letting go of my expectations, entering grief and emptiness, and embracing the cross and lying in the tomb, before resurrection life could be given to me.

Earlier in my life, when I was wandering in dangerous spiritual places, I repeatedly dreamed of being in the wrong classroom, having studied the wrong subjects, and of being unprepared for a test on subjects I had not studied. However, I didn't know how to respond to these warnings. The recurrent dream was potentially a true guide for me, but I lacked a mentor or community to help me explore the right path. It planted in me a suspicion that I was not focused on the right way, and so it helped prepare me for finding my path in the future.

Parker Palmer shares about when he was searching for a vocational direction:

> If I were ever to discover a new direction, I thought, it would
> be at Pendle Hill, a community rooted in prayer, study, and
> a vision of human possibility. But when I arrived and started
> sharing my vocational quandary, people responded with a
> traditional Quaker counsel that, despite their good inten-

tions, left me even more discouraged. "Have faith," they said, "and *way will open*."

"I have faith," I thought to myself. "What I don't have is time to wait for 'way' to open. I'm approaching middle age at warp speed, and I have yet to find a vocational path that feels right. The only way that's opened so far is the wrong way."

After a few months of deepening frustration, I took my troubles to an older Quaker woman well-known for her thoughtfulness and candor. "Ruth," I said, "people keep telling me that 'way will open.' Well, I sit in the silence, I pray, I listen for my calling, but way is not opening. I've been trying to find my vocation for a long time, and I still don't have the foggiest idea of what I'm meant to do. Way may open for other people, but it's sure not opening for me."

Ruth's reply was a model of Quaker plain-speaking. "I'm a birthright Friend," she said somberly, "and in sixty-plus years of living, way has never opened in front of me." She paused, and I started sinking into despair. Was this wise woman telling me that the concept of God's guidance was a hoax?

Then she spoke again, this time with a grin. "But a lot of way closed behind me, and that's had the same guiding effect."[22]

When we seek to discern God's direction, we need to have the humility to accept that sometimes the answer may be "no" or "not yet." Acts 16 tells the story of Paul and those accompanying him on his missionary journey to bear the gospel of Christ; God gives them several "no's" before they receive a "yes":

> They went through the region of Phrygia and Galatia, having been forbidden by the Holy Spirit to speak the word in Asia. When they had come opposite Mysia, they attempted to go into Bithynia, but the Spirit of Jesus did not allow them; so, passing by Mysia, they went down to Troas. During the night Paul had a vision: there stood a man of Macedonia pleading

with him and saying, "Come over to Macedonia and help us."
When he had seen the vision, we immediately tried to cross
over to Macedonia, being convinced that God had called us
to proclaim the good news to them.

Acts 16:6–10

This story of Paul and his band of missionaries omits any details on what form the negative responses from the Holy Spirit took. But the travelers clearly sought God's guidance on their missionary journey, and their plans were blocked. The story tells us that the "yes" came one night to Paul in a vision, which could have been either a dream or an image emerging from deep prayer or meditation. Although the vision came to Paul, the response is consensual, since Paul's companions all were convinced that God had called them to Macedonia for their missionary work.

Let's look at a few examples from my spiritual direction practice and personal life when the *via negativa* became part of discerning situations.

Empty Box

A guided-imagery meditation I have often used in my spiritual guidance practice leads the individual or group on a search for buried treasure.[23] Most of the time the meditator discovers something inside the treasure chest that symbolically represents something he or she values but might be hidden or not always recognized. There are occasions, however, when the meditator visualizes the treasure box but finds it empty. In such cases, the guide provides a safe opportunity for the meditator to explore the *quality* of that emptiness and to discover its wisdom. The emptiness might represent something to be grieved, a treasure that has been lost, misplaced, or depleted. But the empty box may also be a creative container rich with the possibility of new things yet to come. Sometimes the empty treasure box might be an "empty tomb" that no longer contains the radically changed and resurrected new life the person is now living, just like an opened chrysalis indicates that what once was a caterpillar has now transformed into a butterfly.

Barren Ground

Retirement constituted a passage from emptiness to new life for one of my directees. She had just retired from active parish ministry when we first began to meet for spiritual direction. When I asked her whether she had a primary image of what retirement felt like, she visualized a barren field. What had been a rich life of ministry felt finished, and she was anxious about the future: What would she do? Would she be well enough off financially? She trusted that God would be with her but still lacked clarity about what the future held. Months passed, and she and I revisited her primary image and noticed the changes that had occurred. After a while she no longer visualized the ground as barren; it became a fallow field, open and receptive to new life rather than abandoned or a place of waste. Then the field was prepared, and new seeds were planted. She wasn't sure what those seeds were yet; it seemed to her that God was doing the planting. She felt much less anxious about her life. Later she noticed that the seeds had begun to sprout and that new life was quickening below the surface; still, she could not tell what those new things were. She was hopeful. Finally, the plants broke the soil and began to mature—she discovered and claimed her new interests and activities, her newfound financial situation, and her postretirement ways of offering ministry.

> Can you identify significant events in which you have encountered this movement of the *via negativa*? How did it guide or otherwise support you, as well as challenge you to change?

At the beginning of my Christian walk as a young adult, one of my dreams spoke to me of walking by heart and not by sight, of an old life left behind and a new life beginning. The dream had a feel for the wisdom of *via negativa* spirituality:

The Garden (June 7, 1978)

I become aware that I am having a dream and know that the Holy Spirit will become present with me because this is what

I have hoped for in a lucid dream. But with that realization I am fearful and wonder if I will die, for it says somewhere in Scripture that you cannot see God and live. I am blinded immediately upon recognition of my lucidity. Simultaneously, I am gripped gently but forcefully by the heart. It feels like great fingers have grasped me. I try to struggle against the grasp but only stumble around, and it hurts to do so—I feel the pressure of the fingers increase when I resist. I know that it is futile to struggle, and so I relax to the leading of Spirit. I am led in darkness to a garden and regain my sight. I am placed in front of some small trees or large shrubs. A sign states that it was necessary for these plants to die in order to come alive again and flourish.

This dream symbolized for me some of the primary wisdom of the Christian spiritual journey. My encounter with the Divine and the walk I was to make was "by faith and not by sight" (2 Cor. 5:7). I had desired to be led by the Spirit of Christ but was also struggling to "let go and let God" take the lead. The encounter with the Divine firmly led me by the heart, and it hurt me to resist. I think of Paul, then named Saul, hearing the voice of Jesus, "Saul, Saul, why are you persecuting me? It hurts you to kick against the goads" (Acts 26:14). The trees and shrubs in the garden that were now thriving first had to be cut down—suggestions of death and new life in Christ.

Be alert to *via negativa* symbols and events when you come upon them in your search or are engaged in discernment. We learn important things from the way of negation, of blindness or uncertainty, of emptiness or stripping away. Sometimes we must be led into mystery and into that wisdom beyond the rational grasp of our intellect alone but nevertheless accessible by following a path with heart. It is not a comfortable path, but great wisdom may await us.

3 Practices for Inviting the Emergence of Guiding Symbols

MANY PRACTICES ASSIST us in becoming aware of guiding symbols as we engage in discernment and seek direction. I think of these practices as asking God for the gift of guiding symbols. Avoid forcing symbols to appear. Instead, pray for the gift of guiding symbols and invite them to emerge into consciousness from the wisdom deeply planted in our individual and collective depths. Such an approach respects the sacred nature of these gifts.

In this chapter I present a number of practices as examples of the ways we invite and receive God's symbolic communication. I draw most of my examples from my experience with dreams and imagery meditation; I am personally drawn to those practices because of my particular personality and abilities, and it is not intended to diminish the effectiveness and quality of other practices. If the presentation of practices seems uneven, it is simply because I have more experience and knowledge of dreamwork and imagery meditation; you may find other ways of cultivating guiding symbols better suited to your interests and capabilities.

Waiting at the Threshold
Holy Silence
Our dominant culture fears silence, and, unfortunately, much of our worship mirrors that dread of sustained quiet. Cultivating a capacity for holy silence seems countercultural and likely will be resisted and misunderstood. But developing an ability to be silent, allowing hospitable space for the Presence, is an essential practice. In holy silence we wait expectantly at the threshold for a meeting with the Divine. This

kind of hospitable, respectful, holy silence also invites the emergence of our deep interior symbols and their wisdom.

The statement "silence is God's first language, all else is a poor translation" has been variously attributed to the Persian and Afghan mystic Rumi (1207–1273), the Rhineland mystical theologian Meister Eckhart (ca. 1260–ca. 1328), and the Carmelite mystical theologian John of the Cross (1542–1591), as well as some contemporary spiritual teachers. The attachment of such illustrious names to the statement, whether or not they actually said it, underscores the importance of silence as a conduit to spiritual depths and encounter with the Divine. From the desert elders early in Christian history through the development of monastic rules of life, the cultivation of holy silence has been recognized as foundational.

What is your own experience of silence as a part of your spiritual life, its role in discernment, and as a medium for your relationship with the Divine?

What value does your culture or ethnicity place upon silence and its use?

Becoming truly silent is a hard task. So many things conspire to distract us and keep closed the doors and windows to our unconscious depths. Our books, music, work, to-do lists, television and video streams, movies, texting, instant messaging, tweeting, phone conversations, and many more objects and activities support our anxiety about becoming truly silent while waiting for subconscious and unconscious "stuff," along with the Presence, to erupt into our awareness. To become silent is to take a risk and be vulnerable, to ease off being in charge of ourselves the way our little ego feels is manageable. To be truly silent is to become open, awaiting messages from another realm and perhaps even an encounter with the One who is no-thing. What we receive in the silence may feel uncomfortable, even terrifying, revealing hidden things about ourselves and the dwellers in the spiritual world that we would rather not acknowledge. No wonder we so often avoid silence.

But if we desire God's guidance in our lives—and wish to know the deep wisdom the Holy Mystery has for us—this silence is frequently required.[1] "Be still and know that I am God!" (Ps. 46:10a). Cultivating a capacity for holy silence is, therefore, the first and most basic practice. It is prayer itself . . . and the threshold to encounters with the Holy.

The apophatic dimension (negative way) of Christian spirituality cultivated practices of silent prayer beginning with early desert monasticism in the second century.[2] The Eastern church's mystical teachers and theologians give care and attention to hesychastic (quiet) prayer forms that are often called "prayer of the heart," because a simple phrase is repeated aloud or silently in rhythm with the breath. This simple repetitive prayer, such as "Holy God, holy and mighty, holy Immortal One, have mercy on us" or "Lord Jesus Christ, Son of God, have mercy on me, a sinner," coupled with breathing, provides an interior sense of quiet and attentiveness to God.

What is currently called "centering prayer" by its advocates in the Western church has its roots in the fourteenth-century's anonymous English mystical treatise *The Cloud of Unknowing*. With this practice the focus is on a quiet openness to God, without presumption. Whenever the mind wanders, as it frequently will, a focus word gently brings the attention back to that interior quiet and openness to the Divine. Practitioners of centering prayer suggest twenty minutes of silent prayer twice a day.

Spiritual directors are often asked about silent prayer practices. My own counsel is that a short period of silence (a minute or longer) is always good as a preparation for more active forms of prayer and meditation. Many of my directees prefer to have our sessions begin with several minutes of silence to "center down" and for us to open ourselves to the Spirit's presence. Some people prefer more formal times of prolonged silence, engaging in personal and group forms of silently attending to the Divine.

Practices Using Imagination

All of the active practices (kataphatic-affirmative way) that I introduce in this chapter make use of our imagination. The following practices have a particular meditational quality, where we are desiring and inviting God's guidance and wisdom and intentionally imagining and engaging a scene or persona. Note that distinguishing among techniques is fairly arbitrary.

Active Imagination

This practice finds its roots in Jungian psychotherapy, where we engage our inner energies, the archetypes. These archetypes are autonomous personalities with whom we dialogue and from whom we learn. We seek as well to integrate their power into our true selves. Jungian analyst Robert Johnson offers this precaution for active imagination and dreamwork, advice that applies to other deep encounters with the unconscious: be sure to have someone help you, preferably a therapist, a spiritual director, a counselor, or someone else who has experience in this area of personal growth.[3]

Several of my directees have talked about the image of the angel and devil perched on either shoulder whispering in their ears as they try to resolve a moral dilemma. It isn't uncommon to see this depicted in cartoons or other presentations in comedic form. I would often encourage directees to play out this dialogue in the direction session, asking them to give voice to those little beings, listening and considering what they were trying to say to the directee. And I mean it when I say "play," since having a little creative humor and curiosity about the exercise often invites a more productive engagement with these inner personas. Are there desires, anxieties, fears, hopes, temptations, or needs trying to be expressed? Are there deeper truths that need to be considered in working through resolution to the apparent conflict? Is there some reconciliation that can be creatively "negotiated" that honors truths the two sides express?

One of my direction clients suffered for many years with deep clinical depression. She began meeting with me to help her grow into greater wholeness and spiritual health. She told me that in the past she had progressed, guided by a Christian counselor, toward greater healing by getting to know her "inner committee" and thought it might be helpful to begin that work again. We talked this over, and I agreed to continue that work with her as part of her ongoing spiritual direction. She introduced me to her seven or so inner personas; each had names, particular physical characteristics, genders, and ages as well as personalities. When we began, no member of this "inner committee" was behaving in her favor or advocating for her best interests. They were expressing themselves negatively, or at best as passive or overwhelmed beings. We agreed that she would spend a limited time daily in prayerful meditation with one of the personas in the imagined presence of the risen Christ. She believed Jesus Christ would act as a healer and as an advocate for her well-being and wholeness, and, at the same time, he would also be a compassionate presence that could help the persona change over time. As she listened to the persona in the presence of Christ she began to see that it was expressing, in a misdirected way, a concern about her. It might have been a fear of failure, an anxiety about not doing things perfectly, or a diminished sense of self-worth. Slowly, over time, as concerns a persona brought to her were received without judgment and compassionately embraced in the safe presence of Christ, she found that she could remain more and more in the confidence and strength of her mature self. She also noticed that the personas began changing; they were discovering their own gifts that could aid her. Through her prayerful meditations with Christ present as healer and reconciler, members of her inner committee became advocates for her and brought their gifts for integration into her true self.

Inner-child work is a form of active imagination practice in which we engage with that part of our self that is a child, although it can take other forms too, who feels the need for safety and care, healing from hurts, and opportunities for wonder and creative play. I remember being invited to preach at a seminary Eucharist, for the first time since my student years. I was going to be speaking in the presence of teachers that I admired. My growing anxiety became a real impediment to my ability to prepare a homily, and finally I needed to step back and recognize what was happening. I quieted myself and asked God to give me an image for whatever was bothering me and making me feel so anxious. What appeared was a frightened and anxious little boy—a young version of me, Danny. I asked him what was wrong. Danny told me how scared he was to be in the presence of all these brilliant people who were so much smarter than he was, and he was afraid that what he had to say would sound stupid and he would be humiliated. I felt myself hurting for the little guy and told him that I was all grown up and would look out for him; he wouldn't be ashamed of what he/I had to say. Something about facing that fear and anxiety personified in my inner child, and assuming the role of mature protector, helped me claim my adult voice and perspective, freeing me to craft the homily and offer my best to the seminary congregation.

Depth Prayer

Closely related to active imagination is what one of my teachers at the Upper Room Academy, Flora Wuellner, calls depth prayer. In fact, the kind of imaginative prayerful meditation that my client practiced with her inner committee in the presence of Christ offers a fine example of depth prayer. Inviting the presence of Christ, or other symbolic representation of divine Presence, to mediate our interaction with whatever symbolic energies emerge from our subconscious or unconscious (people, animals, plants, and otherwise), provides a healing or integrative opportunity to occur in prayer. New insights and wisdom emerge from such interactions. Working with these inner symbolic energies in the presence of the Divine is truly a light on the path to greater healing and God's shalom/peace.

Depth prayer may take the form of asking God to reveal whatever God wishes, and then waiting, sometimes for an extended time, for images or scenes to emerge. Or it may take the form of a self-led imagery meditation based on a general scenario you have already established. In that case, the technique is different from guided-imagery meditation, described next, only because there is no external guide.

Guided-Imagery Meditation

The practices described above may be self-led, but there is also active imagination or depth prayer guided by someone other than the meditator. Often the experience of first being led by a skilled guide opens the door to later self-led practices of engaging imagination in prayer or meditation. In guided-imagery meditation, the guide makes suggestions, not directives, for the meditator to use in the prayer or meditation experience. The meditator should always feel free to go in a different direction than the guide suggests if it seems right to do so. The control over the movements in the meditation remains with the meditator. The role of the guide is to suggest a scenario and interactions, and to provide a safe and hospitable container for the meditator's experience. The guide can also help the meditator process and reflect upon the meditation once it ends. Sometimes a guide helps someone engage in active imagination—like the little angel and demon sitting on each shoulder and whispering in the person's ear—and the meditator describes to the guide what is occurring during the active imagination session.

As previously mentioned, imagery meditation is far from a new practice. Ignatius of Loyola provided Scripture-based or sacred situational meditations in the sixteenth century. Guided imagery may be useful for both individual and group meditation. It is not uncommon to use guided imagery during a spiritual direction or spiritual companionship session. It also can be very valuable to offer a group, such as a church board and staff, a group-oriented imagery meditation.

Usually in guided-imagery meditations the guide takes the individual or group on some kind of inner journey. It might be a search for hidden treasure, a journey to where the Wise One lives, a meeting with the Healer, or an encounter with the Divine in some other form. Often the meditator is invited to bring back some gift from the meditation. To give you an example of such a journey, during Lent I developed a guided-imagery meditation based on the Gospel of Mark's story of Jesus being baptized and then going into the wilderness to be tempted by Satan. It would be suitable for an individual or for a group to share and reflect upon together. Be sure to pause for reflection after each movement:

God's Love and the Wilderness

> At this time, Jesus came from Nazareth in Galilee and was baptized by John in the Jordan. The moment he came out of the water, he saw the sky split open and God's Spirit, looking like a dove, come down on him. Along with the Spirit, a voice: "You

are my Son, chosen and marked by my love, pride of
my life."

At once, this same Spirit pushed Jesus out into
the wild. For forty wilderness days and nights he was
tested by Satan. Wild animals were his companions,
and angels took care of him.

—Mark 1:9–13 (*The Message*)[4]

1. Close your eyes and take a few slow, full, relaxing
breaths. Let the outer world fade away and awaken to your
inner world.

2. Imagine emerging from a body of water—you are wet
but also warm as you take in a deep fresh breath of air—you
feel refreshed and full of life, full of Spirit.

3. From somewhere beyond *and* deep within you the
Sacred Presence says, "You are my very own child, chosen and
marked by my love. You are the pride of my life." Savor those
words meant for you from the Holy One: "You are mine,
chosen and marked by my love. You are the pride of my life."
Notice what feelings and thoughts emerge as you sit with
being God's beloved daughter or son. If you feel the need to
stay with this sense of God's love, feel free to do so.

4. Others may wish to move to another scene, bringing
with you that sense of God's love. That same spirit of love
and pride in you now pushes you to a wilderness where you
will be tested by another spirit. Look around that wilderness.
What does it look like? What kind of testing happens to you
in your wilderness? What does your tester look like? What
feelings and thoughts emerge about being tested?

5. There are wild animals and angels in your wilderness.
Are wild animals helpful or harmful to you? Be aware of any
wild animal that might appear to you. If it comes to you, feel
free to interact with it. What does it say to you or show you?
What is wild in you and in your life? How do you feel about
those wild parts of you?

6. Who are your angels, the messengers of God's love for you, the ones that take care of you in your wilderness? How do they help you? Do you see any of them now? If so, feel free to interact with that angel.

7. It is time to return to this outer world now, bringing back what you wish from your inner experience of love and the wilderness. Is there something special from your meditation—a word, image, or new insight—that feels important enough to bring back with you?

8. Now slowly take two or three full, relaxed breaths and let your inner world fade. Make your journey back to join the rest of us in this outer world.

When introducing guided-imagery meditation, I mention that we may experience the meditation at various levels of vividness at different times. Sometimes the imagination is deeply engaged and the meditator sees, or hears, the scenario vividly, but at other times he or she may only get a vague interior picture and feelings; still, at other times, the meditator may do more "thinking it through" than entering the scene. I encourage new meditators to suspend judgment about what is a "good" meditation and simply engage it with a willingness to be in the scene in whatever way God gives it to them. Sometimes people simply "go blank" and don't remember anything. I encourage them to allow that without judgment, too. God does not only work with us consciously, so it is possible that something was happening on a deep unconscious level even if the person seemingly fell asleep.[5]

Also, because engaging in this kind of meditation requires healthy ego strength and the capacity to distinguish between inner and outer realities, I don't recommend it for people who deal with mental illness in which a psychotic state might accidentally be induced, or for anyone in an extremely fragile emotional state. They might "think" about the scene and talk with an experienced guide about what develops, keeping the scene or situation somewhat detached, but do not encourage them to imaginatively enter scenes unless accompanied by a therapist who determines that this is an appropriate thing to do. I have heard of rare situations in which a person has a psychotic break with reality and is trapped inside the imaginary story; a skilled therapist or other guide has had to work to bring the person back to reality.

I once led a small group that I knew very well in a guided-imagery meditation at a church I served. What was disclosed to one of the women during her meditation was so powerful that the truth revealed a very fragile personal situation for which she needed significant support and mental-health care. The group provided a setting safe enough for disclosure, and she went on to receive the care that she needed. Both I, as her pastor, and the small group were part of her support system. Caution is required, because serious issues requiring important decisions and/or healing can surface through these powerful practices.

Shamanic Journeying

I recognize that the practices I mention here as "shamanic journeying" may feel strange, weird, or dangerous to some readers. However, the practices for using imagination I have already described are similar in nature, because an inner journey to engage lively images that dwell in the unconscious is the key to exploring spiritual reality. Two generations ago, Episcopal priest and educator Urban T. Holmes spoke of the priesthood as having shamanic roots. Likewise, Morton Kelsey wrote a chapter on the modern shaman and Christian belief in *Transcend: A Guide to the Spiritual Quest.* In writing on spiritual direction in another book, Kelsey noted that the practice can take two levels. One level of spiritual direction is what we normally employ in companioning our clients in reflection on their lives. But he also recognizes a second "shamanistic" level that may need to be employed to help people who have been thrust deeply into the psyche.[6]

Different cultures over thousands of years have used varying techniques for making a trance journey to spiritual worlds. These people have been called by many different names, with the name *shaman* having come originally from a tribal culture in Siberia. Current teachers and writers, such as Tom Cowan and anthropologist Michael Harner, give a generic name of "shaman" or "shamanic practitioner" to describe these inner spiritual journeyers. Usually in the shaman is a desire to bring healing, wisdom, and practical knowledge back from their spiritual journeys. Often a ritual involving drumming or rattling, which may be combined with dance, mediates the journey. Other intentional practices that can induce shamanic journeys include the use of dreams, imagery meditation, chant, fasting, and vigils. I do not advocate the use of psychotropic drugs for these journeys, because drugs can unsafely throw people off balance in various ways.

Traditional shamanic societies recognize three worlds: upper, middle, and lower. The upper and lower worlds are part of the "nonordinary reality" inhabited by spirits, who can be visited for help and guidance. The middle world, where we normally dwell, contains a mixture of spirits and our ordinary material reality. In other words, the middle world includes both our "normal reality," which we usually perceive, and "nonordinary reality," which requires some alteration of consciousness and the power of our imagination to perceive. An array of spiritual beings, some being godlike or angelic beings and others looking like regular humans, inhabit the upper world; these may offer guidance and teaching. Nature beings and spirit animals inhabit the lower world; some of these can be "helper" spirits that assist us in fulfilling the intention of shamanic journeys. It is from the nonordinary reality of the middle world where the greatest need for careful discernment exists. It is here that we may encounter troubled or demonic spiritual beings that exert influence and power upon our "ordinary reality."

At the time of writing this book, I had only made a few journeys into these nonordinary realms using specifically shamanic practices (drumming or rattling). I was not surprised to see two helper spirit animals appear and offer companionship and guidance—not surprised because both "Lion" and "Bear," a beautiful mountain lion and a large brown bear—appropriate to California, where I live—had made multiple appearances in dreams and as primary archetypal symbols before I began my experiential journeys. I carry my vocational identity as a Christian priest as I explore these worlds and build relationships. So, as an example, I have had conversations and shared concerns with my helper animals about human destruction of our ecosystem.

The following reports my first shamanic journey with Lion:

Using the drumming music, I began my inner journey and saw Lion, who was ahead of me. Where Bear in the past was running, Lion has more of a sleek, graceful, walking movement. I can easily follow Lion's lead. We come to a dark area, like a hole, and I follow Lion a long way down a tunnel. I can hardly see, and sometimes Lion growls to help me know he is still with me. As I continue descending I smell the moist richness of earth and deep underground stone. I like the smell—it feels like a place I belong. Eventually the dark, descending passage ends at a cave exit.

I can only vaguely see the land. I immediately thank Lion for being with me and leading me to this world. Lion looks at me with a serene and intent gaze. I ask Lion for a name that I can call him or her. I don't get an answer, so I will just call my friend Lion for now. I ask if I might look him over. (I will use the pronoun "him" until I am clearer about gender.) This mountain lion has a beautiful face and strong, smooth, powerful body. There is a dark brown tip to his tail. I ask if I can see some of the place we are in, and he takes me to a nearby cascade or waterfall that drops about thirty feet to the river. I see some large, beautiful, multicolored trout clustered together.

Lion and I then have a conversation about human devastation of the planet, our toxic pollution that threatens many species. Lion is aware of Jesus as the human manifestation of the Divine and that I am a Christian priest. I talk about how we humans have failed to respond to God's charge for us in the creation myth to care for the garden. I apologize for our failure and acknowledge how important it is for humans to change and reunite with the rest of creation and not set ourselves apart from other forms of life and the Earth.

I ask Lion if he would be willing to accompany me to the upper world, too. I sense that he can and would if I called upon him. I thank him for joining me at times on my walks along the bay as I felt and imagined his presence between the ordinary and nonordinary middle world where I normally live. I ask him to teach me and support me. I admire the archetypal traits that I can draw upon from Lion as a friend. The drumming signaled the "call back," and Lion and I again moved to the entrance of the cave, entered the dark upward passageway, and I returned to ordinary reality.

As limited as my experience has been so far, I already feel drawn into a deeper love relationship with our natural world; as a member of a vast community of living beings, I connect more closely with the Earth as a sacrament of God.[7]

Power of Words

I don't think many of us fully appreciate how powerfully words shape our consciousness. Many of us grew up with the saying, "Sticks and stones can break my bones, but words will never hurt me." Not true. Words directed at us can give life, support, encouragement, and strength, and they can be the source of suffering, shame, wounding, and even death. Words revealing hidden secrets or with the intent of belittlement have brought on suicide. Words withheld may bring confusion, uncertainty, and anxiety to one situation, but space, freshness, or mystery to another circumstance. Words administer the healing balm of forgiveness and open people to new visions and possibilities. Words create order in our world and provide an essential expression and reflection of our life within it.

In this age of instantaneous mass communication, we face new gifts and dangers in our technologies. Being able to contact people immediately through social media networks, texting, and other forms of communication is a great blessing. We can be in touch with people across the world with the push of a button. This gives us an amazing ability to bring people together and to build relationships in ways unimaginable a few generations ago.

And yet, there is a danger of diminishing the quality of relationships, too. Cyber-bullying threatens the well-being of our children. What constitutes a "friend" in social media networking is a mere shadow of that rare and intimate relationship. Sentence construction deteriorates under the social pressures of text messaging, and we should wonder if that loss in quality reflects the way we see our communication partners. A chasm in understanding exists between "word processing" and the potential of the sacred word. In the first Genesis creation story, for example, God speaks, and the cosmos is created. In the second creation story, human beings give names to the various creatures and, with that naming, establish relationships with them. The Gospel of John's prologue starts, "In the beginning was the Word, and the Word was with God, and the Word was God." For Christians, Jesus Christ is the embodied, incarnate Word of God.

God cannot be fully named and so, in our relationship with this divine mystery, cannot be completely contained or controlled. Names for God are always provisional, situational, and never complete. Our relationship to God is always evolving, and so our metaphors and names may speak to a dimension of the Holy One in our life now, in the past, or hoped for in the future, but the language is always limited and changing.

Words hold sacred power. Some of that sacredness has been lost in our rationalist cultural perspective, but we need not be limited to the rationalist understanding. We can reclaim the sacred power of the word. The following spiritual practices focus on the creative and sacred power of words.

Lectio Divina: *Holy Reading*

This devotional and contemplative engagement with Holy Scripture has ancient roots. People seeking spiritual guidance often consulted the desert monastics of the fourth to ninth centuries. They might have asked one of the spiritual elders to give "a word of life that I may live."[8] The advice or counsel often took the form of Scripture given by the elder to the seeker. That Scripture was to be taken into their hearts and meditated upon like a planted seed so that it might grow and help shape them over time. You might draw upon that desert wisdom practice and ask yourself: What short passages of Scripture give meaning and direction to my life?

Benedict of Nursia, in his sixth-century *Rule,* required that his monks practice two hours of *lectio divina* daily. The *Rule* does not prescribe a particular method for engaging Scripture. It just emphasizes the importance of the practice as a way to be spiritually formed continually. The personal practice of formation by Scripture was complemented and supported communally with daily prayer offices—the "liturgy of the hours" such as Vigils, Lauds, Vespers, and Compline—in which Scripture, especially the psalms, were continuously being recited and internalized by the gathered community.

In the twelfth century, Hugh of St. Victor wrote about *lectio divina* as a spiritual exercise consisting of reading, reflection, prayer, practice (*operatio*), and contemplation. Probably influenced by Hugh of St. Victor, Guigo the Carthusian provided what has become the classic movements of *lectio divina*: reading (*lectio*), meditation (*meditatio*), prayer (*oratio*), and contemplation (*contemplatio*). Prior Guigo wrote:

> We read a text of scripture or serious poetry or religious writing. We meditate to enter deeply into the text's meaning. In prayer we respond to God in the light of this meaning. In contemplation we rest simply in the presence of God, needing no further words. Reading, as it were, puts the food into the mouth. Meditation chews it and breaks it up. Prayer extracts its flavor. Contemplation is the sweetness itself which gladdens and refreshes.[9]

In practice, these movements are not always sequential, and they are not likely to take equal amounts of time. As with the spiritual discernment cycle, it is helpful to see the movements of *lectio divina* as a dance with God. Often this way of engaging Scripture—or, as Guigo adds, serious poetry or spiritual or religious writing—begins with the holy silence we discussed earlier. Since *lectio divina* is a spiritual practice, we should want to silently open ourselves to the Divine. We give quiet consent to the Holy One's ability to encounter us through the words, and we prepare ourselves with the hope that our open desire will be met by the One who desires us.

And so, typically, the movement of *lectio* is to read slowly and with openness and wonder, noticing when something seems to shimmer for you and gets your attention. You are looking for the active and creative Word amid the text. This kind of reading aims not as much for *information* as for our spiritual *formation*; it is not an exercise in critical study of Scripture but rather in devotional engagement with the Divine through sacred literature. (There certainly is an important place for formal study, too, in spiritual life, but the focus is different.) In *lectio divina* you take a risk inasmuch as you relinquish ego control to enter more fully into the possibility of Divine encounter. Because you become vulnerable, you may also resist the encounter. When you notice particular energy around a word, phrase, verse, image, or scene, you have probably met *the Word*. This is the place to dwell for a time of *meditatio.*

In *meditatio* you meditate on the possible meanings of the text as it applies to you now. What might the text mean for you? What is God trying to say to you? You may notice the stirring of feelings or thoughts from that word, phrase, verse, or image. These feelings or thoughts may feel positive or negative. The desert elders spoke of this meditation as rumination—like a cow chewing cud, swallowing, and then chewing again. You might chew on this text again and again, finding other associated possibilities or feelings. You may enter, as with Ignatian meditation, into the text's scene and explore it. This movement is primarily "thinking about" and exploring possible personal meaning. Eventually it moves deeper and leads you to another movement that engages the whole of yourself.

Oratio is not a nice, tidy, clean, little prayer experience. It is messy, gut-level prayer. It is wrestling with God in the meaning to which the text calls you, or it is making love to the Divine (and vice versa) as longing and desire are released in your bones. This movement uses the insights from your meditation to begin praying through whatever you need to in order to come to terms with what you believe God wants you to be or do. It calls for trust, vulnerability, and honesty with God.

This prayer may bring you to face personal fears, wounds, a sense of inadequacy, or guilt; or, your prayer could be an exhilarating time of discovery or deep questioning; or, it may even be a time when you have to let go of an image of God that you have outgrown or an image of yourself that no longer contains sufficient truth for you. This prayer movement may endure for only a short time or last for days or longer. Stay with this form of prayer as long as necessary, and it is likely that knowledge of what you are to do or how you are to be will emerge. And with that knowing, you may move to contemplation.

Contemplatio is a prayer state that often emerges with resolution, some acknowledgment on a deep level, of what you have been called into by this text and how you will respond. It is experienced as a deep peace and rest in the presence of God. Images may sometimes surface—perhaps a memory of being gently held by a loved one. In this contemplative state you once again know who you are in relationship to God and rest in the assurance of God's love for you. Do not move too quickly from this state if it is given to you—enjoy the gift of being loved.

The time will come when you can take the fruit of this process into your life. In a real sense, the "living and active Word" (Heb. 4:12) has come to you, and in a mysterious and transformative way has brought about change, conversion, or deepened sense of direction. You now bear this Word anew in the world.

The practice of holy reading need not be restricted to Scripture. You can also read poetry and literature reflectively, and, in the process, encounter powerful symbols that speak of God's desires for you. This basic process applies to any situation in which we have the opportunity to ask where God is and what resources we might call forth.

Group Forms of Lectio Divina

Holy reading also occurs in community groups. A leader can simply read a passage aloud once or twice, then provide an extended period of silence during which group members engage the passage quietly. After the silence, the group leader asks the members where the passage took them in their personal meditation and prayer.

In another popular and effective method of group meditation on Scripture, one member reads the passage aloud, the group observes a short silence, and then all members report what word, phrase, or image in the passage particularly struck them. The leader then asks another

member to read the passage again—perhaps using a different translation—followed by another period of silent reflection, after which everyone reports on how the passage connected to their lives. Finally, the
leader asks a third group member to read through the passage, perhaps
with a third translation, followed by another short reflective silence,
after which all members share what they think God is inviting them to
be or do based on all that they said and heard. The leader then may ask
prayer for each other as a way of closing the group.

Three Ways into Scripture Meditation

If we look at the *meditatio* or meditation movement of *lectio divina*,
we understand that meditation with Scripture uses primary faculties
of thinking, imagining, and feeling. Any of these three ways of engaging Scripture helps illuminate our path. You might discover that
one or two of these ways work better for you because of your internal
"hardwiring."

Thinking. We approach Scripture by discursive meditation, using
words and our ability to reason. Here we may ask ourselves the following questions:

- ▸ What is going on in the reading?
- ▸ What questions arise for me?
- ▸ What does the passage mean to me?
- ▸ How will I respond? What do I resolve to do or be because of
  this reading?

Imagining. This is an Ignatian approach, in which we enter into the
Scripture using our imagination:

- ▸ Visualize the scene as clearly as possible.
- ▸ If I were one of the biblical characters, what would it be like to
  be him, or her, or it?
- ▸ If I were there, what would I feel, say, and do?
- ▸ What do I take from this to apply to my life?

Feeling. With this approach, we focus on our affective response to Scripture and look for intuitive wisdom:

▸ What feelings arise as I read this passage?
▸ Do I feel consonance or dissonance with the text?
▸ Where do these feelings take me in understanding my present relationship to God, myself, and others?
▸ What might God be asking me to change, deepen, affirm, or work on?

Creative Writing and Personal Narrative

This is, of course, such a vast subject that I will do little more than introduce it as a possible practice to bring to consciousness guiding symbols for spiritual discernment and direction. Some people create their own psalms, poems, written prayers, or stories. Powerful images may emerge from such a deep and creative source that they seem to come from your soul.

Some poetry forms are short and structured. *Haiku* traditionally consists of three lines of up to seventeen syllables using a pattern such as 5 + 7 + 5. *Cinquain* poems consist of five lines based on the following number of syllables per line: 2 + 4 + 6 + 8 + 2. A quick search on the Internet yields many suggestions for writing your own psalms and for writing short prayers called "collects" (pronounced with the accent on the first syllable), which normally focus on one particular theme and share a basic form: address to God, asking God for something (petition), a statement of aspiration ("so that we/I may. . ."), and final praise (doxology), often in the name of Jesus Christ.

Some people create spiritual autobiographies, for which there are many formats. The Upper Room Academy #5, which I attended in 1988–90, suggested a format for sharing parts of our stories in our covenant group, a format I have sometimes used with a directee when we first meet. In this structure, the narrator considers each decade of his or her life with the following or similar questions to guide their reflection:

▸ Who were the significant people at this time?

- ▸ What were the situations of greatest pain?
- ▸ What were the situations of greatest joy?
- ▸ What were the "sacred moments"? How did I experience God at that time?
- ▸ What images or titles best summarize these different periods?

This kind of review brings to the surface themes that continue to develop, as well as guiding symbols from both God and significant events. All may shed light on the present path.

Sometimes directees and small-group members bring in photos of people (and of themselves at different ages) or memorabilia that enhance their narrative. I often encourage them to think of their story as their personal, developing gospel. Together we make connections between their stories and the sacred stories of Scripture. Although not necessarily written, these life stories can elicit profound themes and guiding symbols, many of which had remained hidden.

Spiritual Journaling

We can benefit from Christian journal-keepers throughout the centuries. Egeria, a woman on pilgrimage in the fourth century, kept a journal of her travels through the Holy Lands; this record provides an invaluable source for modern liturgical study. *The Imitation of Christ* by Thomas à Kempis in the early fifteenth century remains a very popular devotional classic from the *devotio moderna* movement. Dag Hammarskjöld, the second Secretary-General of the United Nations, labored for global peace during the dangerous times of the 1950s and early 1960s. He died in a plane crash while making his fourth trip to the Congo in 1961. His famous journal, *Markings*, published posthumously in 1963, became a contemporary spiritual classic.

Many books and articles have been written about spiritual journaling.[10] My own practice of journaling includes many of my dreams going back to the 1970s, significant events that I want to reflect upon, prayers and meditations, notes from spiritual exercises I have practiced, concerns and wonderings, occasions of grief or joy, records of events while traveling and feelings evoked by those events, and primary symbols and themes as they emerge in my life. Many other uses for a spiritual journal can be incorporated into your practice.

One journaling exercise invites you into an imaginative meeting and dialogue with someone—a saint, a wisdom figure, a historical leader, Jesus, or God. Write your portion of the dialogue with your dominant hand, then use your nondominant hand to write the responses from the one you are meeting in your meditation. Many find it spiritually helpful to write letters to God and to imagine God's response, writing that response back to yourself.

For some, drawing in their journals offers a creative and imaginative way to meditate. Drawing an image that emerges from a dream or active imagining explores its meaning and can uncover its potential message. There is no limit to the ways your journal can explore your spiritual life and evoke important symbols and images, drawing from the unconscious and the imaging side of the brain.

Art

When we consider drawing in a journal, we open up yet another area of possible resources for discovering guiding symbols: *art*. Art in all its breadth comes laden with symbolic value, both for those engaged in the creation of art and for those who receive art and interact with it. Here, in brief, are ways that various media help elicit guiding symbols.

Sculpture

Some people practice sculpture as professional artists. There is something wonderful about seeing into a block of wood or stone and birthing a new image. We experience the symbolic power of sculpture when we imagine the Statue of Liberty. What might this magnificent statue evoke? What does it say about our national aspirations? On the pedestal base of this massive sculpture we find a poem by Emma Lazarus, "The New Colossus," containing some of the most moving phrases related to American ideals ever expressed:

> Not like the brazen giant of Greek fame,
> With conquering limbs astride from land to land;

Here at our sea-washed, sunset gates shall stand
A mighty woman with a torch, whose flame
Is the imprisoned lightning, and her name
Mother of Exiles. From her beacon-hand
Glows world-wide welcome; her mild eyes command
The air-bridged harbor that twin cities frame.
"Keep ancient lands, your storied pomp!" cries she
With silent lips. "Give me your tired, your poor,
Your huddled masses yearning to breathe free,
The wretched refuse of your teeming shore.
Send these, the homeless, tempest-tost to me,
I lift my lamp beside the golden door!"[11]

In our time, when we hotly debate immigration issues and borders, when detention facilities house many undocumented adults and children who aspire to live in this nation, the Statue of Liberty stands as a powerful guiding symbol. A group of us from various churches and community organizations gathers monthly for a vigil at a regional detention facility that detains 250 or more undocumented adults, many for simple civil infractions. At the beginning of each vigil, we mention the Statue of Liberty and hear the words, "Give me your tired, your poor . . ."

Many of us are less gifted in creating sculpture but can still engage in similar practices. Pick up a lump of clay. Relax as you playfully work it with your hands. What form takes shape? What does the form say to you about your life?

Collage

Some sculptors take "things" and weld them together to create a new object. We can do a similar playful practice as an individual or as a group by cutting out pictures from magazines that attract us and pasting them on a big sheet, thus creating a collage. What does the collage tell us? I like to see (similar to *lectio divina*) what catches my attention and "shimmers," rather like the way a person panning for gold looks for the nuggets amidst the slurry of sand and pebbles. Once again, the symbols that stand out can guide us toward discernment and wisdom, both individually and as a community.

Drawing, Painting, and Photography

We do not need to be artistically skilled to draw or paint our spiritual and creative life. Sometimes just doodling releases something significant from our unconscious. In small-group settings or group retreats I often encourage drawing as a way of exteriorizing a key image following a guided-imagery meditation, or as a way of working with a dream. In the earlier example about searching for buried treasure, I often give participants the opportunity to draw the box and its contents. In another form of guided meditation, in which I lead people to a meeting with Christ or a holy wisdom figure, I suggest that the meditator might receive a gift. We then draw the gift as part of debriefing.

I have led people and been a participant in drawing personal mandalas. "What symbols emerge for you when you consider what brings a sense of wholeness in your life?" is the question I use to lead into drawing a mandala, which is a symbolic representation of wholeness. Often a mandala has symmetry, and typically uses a circle and/or four directions, and one or more central images. Although mandalas are largely associated with the spiritual practice of Buddhist sand painting, they show up across time and cultures. In Christianity, a cross is often used as the basis of a mandala. So an exercise in creating a mandala could go like this: *Draw a large circle and then divide the circle into four quadrants by making a cross. In each of the quadrants draw a symbol for something that is a very important element in giving you balance and wholeness in your life.*

For a time in the late 1980s I felt that there was a mandala "out there" waiting for me to discover; I intuitively knew it was waiting, that it would hold profound meaning, and that I would know it when I saw it. For months, wherever I went, I felt a need to be alert for the mandala awaiting me. During this period, I was engaged to Ruth, and we took a trip from Michigan to visit her family in New Jersey for the first time. While there we took a commuter train to Manhattan for some sightseeing. We visited the Episcopal Diocese of New York's Cathedral Church of St. John the Divine, the largest freestanding Gothic cathedral in the world, conceived as a "house of prayer for all people."

We walked down the nave of the church—long enough to hold four football fields end-to-end—and walked up to the high altar. Turning back toward the narthex (entrance lobby) of the cathedral, I was stunned by what I saw. There was my mandala! In my memory, I saw a beautiful, round, stained-glass depiction of Earth as seen from space. What I *actually* saw was the magnificent, circular Rose Window that shows Christ at the center with angels, evangelists, and New and Old Testament prophets radiating outward in concentric circles. Apparently the design and color triggered in my imagination a vision of Earth.

The Earth is my symbol of wholeness; it is my mandala. It is a whole, living system, the complex organism that we might call Gaia, to which we belong as one species among countless others. It is also God's beautiful creation, and those with the eyes for the sacred see it as a sacrament of the Divine. I am a child of the Earth, as we all are, and yet we have the great ability in this time to see it in its fullness from the "heavens" of space. One of our Eucharistic liturgies shares the vision of "this fragile earth, our island home." This view of the Earth from outer space was as significant a shift in perspective as Copernicus's understanding of the Earth revolving around the sun. Do we love and care for the Earth as much as God who created and loves it? Seven centuries ago, Julian of Norwich had a vision of God gently, tenderly, protectively holding the Earth and all creation—like a little hazelnut—in the palm. Do we demonstrate that same tenderness and care? Do we exercise that will to protect and cherish it?

Photography can also become spiritual practice. Looking through a lens and focusing attention on a subject—or viewing the picture that another person has taken—can provide the platform for meditation. Do we see something that tightly focuses our attention? Or opens us to a wide view? Does a subject or situation capture our attention, and where does that take us in our internal processing and meaning-making? Certainly, viewing a painting can also provide a *visio divina* meditation.

Icons

Western Christianity has only relatively recently encountered the power of iconography from Coptic, Greek, and Russian Christian sources. When we lived in the Chicago area there was a special exhibit at one of their great museums on Russian icons. We brought our young son with us to see this exhibit. The area where the icons were on display was darkened, and the lighting was dimmed to protect them. As we moved slowly past each of these "windows into heaven," our young son became more and more disturbed. We asked him what was happening. He replied that the eyes of the people in the icons were alive and following him.

Those who create ("write")[12] icons often use a perspective unusual to the Western viewer, called a "reverse perspective" or "Byzantine perspective." In this perspective we may feel drawn into the icon's frame of reference, its reality, rather than drawing it into ours. Since icons often provide a symbolic representation of Christ or a saint, being with an icon in prayer or meditation can evoke a powerful experience of presence with the Holy. A dialogue with Christ or a saint through an icon window into heaven may provide special insight when engaged in spiritual discernment. You might practice being with an icon similar to engaging Scripture in *lectio divina*.

Audio-Visual Arts

Movies and television powerfully depict our cultural symbols and concerns, our modern myths, fears, and hopes. From 1999–2006 the television series *West Wing* gave a largely positive portrayal of the American political system and governance, focused on the fictitious Democrat administration of President Josiah "Jed" Bartlet and his staff in the West Wing of the White House. In contrast, the subsequent years of fierce political antagonism between parties, increased polarization, and legislative gridlock have produced the bitingly cynical portrayal of national politics in the Netflix series *House of Cards*, which premiered in 2013. The series, based on a BBC series in 1990 of the same name, centers on the career of fictitious Democrat House Majority Whip Frank Underwood, portrayed as vengeful, cunning, scheming, avaricious, and of highly questionable morals. Where Bartlet represented the able use of the art of politics to achieve the common good, Underwood portrays a shadowy, conniving power broker in search of self-interest. These two examples show how values and power can be approached in the American political arena and how television and movies can expose us to social, political, and spiritual issues in our time. We need to evaluate the quality of what is represented and how we are to respond in light of our own values as people seeking faithful lives in the midst of political dynamics and social issues.

Churches can provide rich opportunities for people by viewing movie or television shows together and then hosting a discussion exploring the underlying theological or spiritual themes. A series of structured and candid conversations arose in my church about racism and our parishioners' firsthand experiences. The congregation is mostly white but also includes people of color (African American, Latina, Asian American). Hearing testimony about racism, within our own church as well as in the larger social context, from our peers—and then in small table groups reflecting further on issues brought out in the talks—offered a powerful time of community-wide formation and prayer.

About a year and a half later some significant events occurred. A number of protests and demonstrations erupted around the nation following the acquittal of George Zimmerman in the killing of African American seventeen-year-old Trayvon Martin and the coincidental release of the movie *Fruitvale Station* about the killing of another young black man named Oscar Grant by BART (Bay Area Rapid Transit) police officer Johannes Mehserle in the San Francisco Bay area on New Year's Day in 2009. On a Sunday following these events we had prayer and conversation on racism and violence after our main worship service.

The following Saturday about twenty members of our church went to see *Fruitvale Station* together at a local theater. After viewing the movie, we walked back to the church and spent another hour and a half in prayer, processing our feelings about the movie. This led to further candid discussion about racism and violence with an expressed desire to find ways to continue our conversations and move toward actions designed to influence our social structures.

With regard to communal spiritual discernment, we find ourselves at the early stages of the discernment cycle. Our personal and group conversations, viewing the movie together, and hearing of further incidents of racial violence in our nation—all have made us aware that this is an important issue for us. We have begun exploring the question of where God is calling us to action as a church. Strategic planning considerations are coalescing around racial inequality and our particular situation and resources in the Berkeley area. So, as a community, we are exploring ways to respond. In an organic movement within the parish, a growing number of parishioners lead in joining with other organizations and churches in vigils for detained immigrants. Some parishioners are taking additional action in support of those facing deportation. Also, a significant number of the parish (lay and clergy) joined in a protest organized by Berkeley-area churches in the wake of several police-involved killings of unarmed black men across the country. So, while some responses have occurred after discernment, it is also very likely that a more comprehensive project will develop in response to an important social issue and to local needs.

Music and Song

A young man I once knew was in a serious relationship and considering the possibility of marriage. As his relationship developed, he noticed that the tune of a folk song from his childhood—"Billy Boy"—kept playing in his head. Eventually he recalled the words of the song:

> Oh where have you been Billy Boy, Billy Boy?
> Oh where have you been darling Billy?
> I have been to seek a wife, she's the joy of my life;
> She's a young thing and cannot leave her mother.

That last line suddenly illuminated his situation. For a while he had been subconsciously feeling a growing concern about his girlfriend's relationship to her mother. That relationship seemed too enmeshed to allow adequate space for their relationship to flourish. When he tried to address his concern, his girlfriend broke off the relationship, probably for the best.

One time a parishioner came to see me. He said that he felt very inadequate about prayer and wanted to learn more about how to offer prayer. I asked him when he felt he was most connected to God and the creative power of the Spirit, when he felt most alive. Suddenly he lit up. He said he felt most connected and alive when he played jazz at his keyboard. We wondered together if he prayed through his fingers as he made music.

Music, song, hymnody, and sacred chant offer strong opportunities for connecting to God and holy wisdom. One of our church's small groups focused on a form of *musica divina*, a modification of the *lectio divina* process that uses hymns and other forms of music to evoke divine direction in members' lives. What do the sounds and lyrics illuminate about their life and the part God plays in their lives?

During sabbatical time with my wife in England at a theological college in the tiny village of Cuddesdon in Oxfordshire, we took many walks in the rural pasture land. The tune "Jerusalem" by Sir Hubert Parry often played quietly on my mind as an undertone to my walking reflections, along with William Blake's final lines to his poem, "Till we have built Jerusalem, / in Englands green & pleasant Land."

At one time during this sabbatical, we made a pilgrimage to the Isle of Iona in Scotland and spent a week with that community's Wild Goose music group. I find one of their chants powerfully evocative for me, and I often share it with spiritual direction groups. The simple lyrics are:

> Take, O take me as I am;
> summon out what I shall be.
> Set your seal upon my heart
> and live in me.

We later took another pilgrim journey, this time to the ecumenical monastic community of Taizé in France. Their spiritual chants have touched the world with their prayerful, meditative quality alongside the simple beauty of the community's contemplative form of worship. Such music and chant opens space deep within me and inclines my soul to wait upon the sacred mystery of the Presence.

Body Knowing

There is a danger that the more we become immersed in a rationalistic and technologically centered world, the more we become distanced and detached from our bodies. And yet we are embodied beings, and it does us well to attend and receive the wisdom of our bodies, which, when integrated with our emotions, feelings, instincts, and movements, provide important knowledge. Christianity has suffered much from suspicion of our bodies and the material life. Yet Christians believe that God so loved us and all of creation as to become a human being, taking on flesh, and becoming one of us in history as Jesus of Nazareth. There are spiritual practices that respect and value that body dimension. Here are just a few, and I expect that you will have others.

Body Meditation

Back in the late 1980s, Flora Wuellner led me in my first meditation designed to help me listen to my body as a messenger of God. She asked our class at the Upper Room Academy to quietly scan our bodies, noticing places of tightness or constriction as well as places of energy and expansion. While scanning my body, I noticed tightness and dull pain in the muscles in my neck. I asked myself, "Who or what is a pain in my neck?" Immediately the image of one of my parishioners and her abrasiveness came to my mind. I knew then that when I returned from my session at the academy, I needed to address some things with her. My body was a truth-teller, and I needed to listen to the wisdom it had for me.

Focusing

The psychotherapeutic technique of Eugene Gendlin yields a body-knowing practice called "focusing" or "bio-spiritual focusing," essentially a compassionate communicative relationship with your body and its sensations. In focusing, you attend to whatever feelings you become aware of, become present with the feeling in a compassionate and caring way, and listen for whatever your body might tell you about your life. Often when you give this kind of focused attention to your body and the feelings that arise, and when you befriend the feeling and listen to what it has to say, a shift occurs. This process is closely related to the meditation I mentioned above on listening to our body as a messenger of God.

Yoga, Qigong, Tai Chi

These are wonderful integrative practices, bringing into unity our body, mind, and spirit. Yoga-breathing practices both calm and energize. When I practice yogic breathing, I recall that in Hebrew the word *ruach* means spirit, breath, and wind. In the creation story, God breathes into the human form and gives life to the human being. So too in Ezekiel's vision of the "valley of the dry bones," the Lord God commands: "Come from the four winds, O breath, and breathe upon these slain, that they may live" (Ezek. 37:9b). *Ruach* is that divine animating force that gives life. The very act of breathing is a communion with and through the divine Spirit, the most primal of prayers. No wonder early Christian mystics in *hesychastic* (quiet) prayer practices would teach connecting the rhythm of breathing with simple, repetitive prayer such as:

> Holy God,
> Holy and Mighty,
> Holy Immortal One,
> Have mercy upon us.[13]

Yoga postures and poses (*asanas*) require focus, concentration, and visualization of the posture. There are poses that I never would have thought I could achieve, but over time, with practice and visualization, I surprised myself, realizing the unity of body and imagination. I tend to be a "head" type person, and on the personality typology called Enneagram I identify myself as a 5-Observer. We 5s are often so in our heads that we ask, "What body?" So to practice yoga—and the Chinese

practices I will shortly describe—became important for my wholeness and for schooling me in attending to my body as a conduit of wisdom.

Qigong and Tai Chi derive from ancient Chinese medicine and Taoist philosophy. Tai Chi became the martial-art form of Qigong movements. Qigong can mean "life energy" or "spirit play," and when I am engaged in those movements, matched with breathing, I often feel like I am in a meditative state. Indeed, in some ways I feel like I move in a slow and graceful dance with the Spirit around and within me. I noticed that some forms of Qigong evoke particular awareness and offer me certain insights, whether they are designed to do that or not. For example, there is one form called "pushing a log into the soft earth," and its movements downward and upward often have me ask, "What am I pushing down in my life? What is trying to rise up?" I often receive a quick, intuitive insight, coupled with those questions.

One time my wife and I struggled to discern our readiness to move if a particular job she was considering were offered. We decided to take a retreat together to do some focused discernment around that situation. While apart for most of each retreat day, we came together in the evening to share the results of our reflections. I had serious concerns about relocating so far from our adult children and family, and Ruth shared that concern. We also questioned whether I would be able to build up a practice as a spiritual director again and find a place to help train others in that ministry.

One afternoon during our retreat I was engaged in an eighteen-part form that blends Tai Chi and Qigong. I came to the movement called "wild goose flying," a powerful, fluid, slow motion in which you raise your arms and hands above your head while inhaling and going up on your toes, then slowly bring both arms and feet down while exhaling. The movement is similar to a "complete breath" in yoga, repeated slowly six or more times. Unexpectedly I envisioned myself soaring up high above a pond on strong wings. I felt surprised that the movement and vision evoked from my body a sudden and amazing clarity about relocating if the job were offered to my wife. In a flash of inspiration, I felt completely confident that God's grace would accompany us and

things would open up to practice my ministry, too, if this job was to be hers and felt right for her.

Thin Times and Places

For many millennia, human beings understood the universe as three-tiered with an intermediate realm that provided correspondence between the realm of Earth and the high heavens of the gods. The rise of the age of reason in the twelfth century, continuing with the Enlightenment and the empirical focus of the scientific method, saw the gradual replacement of that view with just two tiers and the elimination or minimization of the intermediate realm. We can be grateful for the wonderful advances in science and technology that are a product of this latter view. However, the objectivist-rationalist understanding that modernism has produced can be too narrow and limited an approach to reality (or realities). Postmodernism now suggests that reality is a social construction. A new cosmology emerges, a cosmology influenced by quantum physics that understands the fluid rather than fixed nature of the universe. We now learn of the creativity of chaos, the interplay of energy, and the strange nature of subatomic matter. String theory even posits multiple universes. I am not a physicist and make no claim to understand all of this with anything but a surface knowledge, but, increasingly, writers and teachers in spirituality and Christian theology point out the parallels between mystical theology, other ancient wisdom traditions such as Taoism, and these new scientific theories. We live in an era in which we can renew some of the latent wisdom in the old view that there is an intermediate realm of spiritual reality, and that we should pay attention to our "inner intermediate realm" for symbolic communication and direction. The Enlightenment freed us from the bondage to superstition, but now we have the opportunity to retrieve the wisdom baby that we threw out with the bathwater.

Many cultures retain the remnants of ancient spiritual understandings of those practices and places where the correspondence between the earthly realm and the Divine seems particularly transparent and the boundaries are especially "thin." As I mentioned earlier, my wife and I made a pilgrimage to the Isle of Iona in the lower Hebrides off the

coast of Scotland, reputed to be such a "thin" place in Celtic Christian spirituality since St. Columba and his twelve companion monks arrived from Ireland in the sixth century. At Iona you find relics from ancient monastic communities—high stone crosses, carved grave slabs, ruins, and a cemetery going back to the ninth century. All evoke the dedicated souls that lived there before us . . . and the continuing Presence that holds us all in communion.

But we do not necessarily need to make a major pilgrimage to a sacred location to discover that the boundary has been breached between the spiritual and material realms. In this section we look at practices that help us connect with the wisdom and insight that "thin" times and places may have for us.

Liturgies and Holy Days

Many years ago as a parishioner at St. Thomas' Church in Battle Creek, Michigan, I was worshiping with others on the Sunday following All Saints' Day. I followed the line of parishioners going to the sanctuary to receive communion and returned to my seat. I watched a long, continuing line of communicants moving forward to receive communion and then returning as I had done. As I sat there, the separation of the present place and time faded, and I was caught in the wonder of contemplating the multitude who had received communion . . . and the multitude that will be part of this communion of Christ in generations to come. The awareness that I am one little part of such a vast company receiving God's grace in this sacramental ritual was, and is, for me a vision of profound belonging.

This recognition that we are bound together—the living and the dead—shifts the doctrine of the "communion of saints" from a sterile and detached theological construct to a deeply moving, felt reality in times of prayer and meditation. Certainly the All Saints' Day themes, support from a great cloud of witnesses and remembrance of those remarkable saints who shaped and witnessed to the Christian faith, offers an opportunity for integrating head and heart. All Souls' Day—in which the remembrance moves to the dead who are known to us and influenced our lives—also blurs the boundary between life and death. In our present parish, we decorate the side chapel in the style of a Mexican *ofrenda*, honoring the Day of the Dead. We begin on All Saints' Day and continue until Advent. Parishioners bring photos and other memorabilia of loved ones to remember and honor them in light of our hope in God's continuing love.

On one occasion during our sabbatical, my wife and I were in Oxford for an overnight visit on All Souls' Day and All Saints' Sunday. On All Souls' Day we took a walking tour of some of the colleges. Then, because I am fan of Charles Williams's novels, we visited his grave in Holywell Cemetery. That evening we planned on attending a performance of Gabriel Fauré's *Requiem* at New College only to discover, to our delight, that we would not just be part of an audience listening to a performance, but we would be part of a community gathered for worship in a full solemn Holy Eucharist. We had begun the day in prayer together remembering those we loved that were now dead, and now we brought them again to our prayers during the Eucharist. We ended the evening by going for dinner at the Eagle and Child pub, a favorite hangout for the Inklings, the Oxford literary circle that had included Williams, C. S. Lewis, and J. R. R. Tolkien. At the pub we sat next to a corner shrine (of sorts) with pictures of Lewis and Tolkien, with other Inklings memorabilia. We toasted the Inklings, including Charles Williams, and reflected on the richness of that All Souls' Day in which we had felt the power of spiritually thin space and time. That night I had a dream:

A Message for Ruth
(night of All Souls' Day, November 3, 2013)

Ruth and I are in a large house that seems somewhat familiar, and she is asleep. I notice that there is a voice message on the phone, and so I listen to it. It is from her father, and he is telling Ruth that he had arrived earlier than expected but not to worry because Stephen picked them up and brought them home.

I told Ruth about my dream, saying that I had a voice message from her father telling her not to worry, that they are all "home." Ruth's father, her brother Stephen, and her sister Priscilla had died in recent years. That dream, especially coming at this All Souls' and All Saints' "thin" time, was a great comfort for her, hearing that they were all "home" and for her not to worry.

These reflections about All Saints' and All Souls' Days are just examples of the potential of holy days and liturgical rites to provide spiritual thin times. The words and actions in the Holy Eucharist offer an opportunity to experience a thin time. When Ruth and I were looking forward to celebrating our marriage, my grandmother Lyon was nearing the end of her life. She told us that she was afraid that she wouldn't be able to live long enough to be with us at our marriage, and she felt very sorry to not be there. In final conversations with her, we each acknowledged our sadness that she would not be able to be physically present with us at our service. However, we also told her that we believed she would be spiritually present, especially during the *Sanctus* in the Eucharistic Prayer, for we pray in that part of the liturgy that we join "together with Angels and Archangels and with all the company of heaven" in praising our holy God. When the marriage occurred, we mentioned to each other that we had felt her presence blessing us.

I had another grandmother with whom my relationship was complicated and largely negative. After she died, I attended her funeral, where her body was displayed in an open casket. She had been such a powerful and forceful figure in our family that I had a moment's irrational fear that she would start breathing and rise up out of her casket. Well, several months went by, and, while driving one day on a county road, my mind turned to her and I began praying for her. Suddenly I was struck by the profound understanding that she was now in the nearer healing presence of God, and that what she could not receive during her lifetime was now being given to her in that loving and healing Presence. Something shifted in me—my own inner healing and compassion for her emerged in a new way, ushering in a new relationship that crossed the boundary of death and life.

Sacred Journeys

As you can see, sometimes the journey we make is wholly internal by prayer, meditation, liturgical rite, or some other means of cultivating an awareness of thin times when guiding symbols and direction can break through. But there are also external practices that help us become aware of God's direction. We now turn our attention to some of those practices.

Contemplative Walk

Also called a "Gospel Walk," a contemplative walk is a meditative way of walking, looking, and listening for God's message. It is not unusual during a retreat, which we will soon discuss, for the leader to send retreatants into the natural surroundings to look for things that "speak to them" about something in their lives. Sometimes people bring back an object (a leaf, stone, piece of wood, etc.) that memorializes some insight they received while on the contemplative walk.

People might also be sent on a neighborhood walk after reading from Scripture to look for something that connects to the passage. This links *lectio divina* with a contemplative walk. Another option? While walking, follow the process of *lectio divina:* open to some event or object during the walk that serves as a "sacred text," something that catches one's attention and initiates the movements of meditation, prayer, and contemplation.

One can also, as one walks, look for and respond to Christ in the faces of people. In one of the Episcopal Church's baptismal promises, we say that, with God's help, we will "seek and serve Christ in all persons." I am told that a Russian Orthodox greeting similar to exchanging the peace in our Eucharistic liturgy is, "In your eyes I see the face of Christ." So we might practice a contemplative openness in our daily travels, thus encountering Christ in and through the people we meet.

Labyrinth Walk

A labyrinth provides a ritual journey in a dedicated location. Unlike a maze, labyrinths are not designed for you to get lost and reach dead-ends, but rather to take you on a meditative journey. Moving through a labyrinth involves distinct movements: entering the labyrinth, walking a looping passage with many turns—sometimes toward the center and sometimes toward the outer boundary—finally reaching the center, where many will pause for a while, then journeying back to exit. You might intentionally bring a question with you as you walk a labyrinth, or you may simply be prayerfully open to what the walk evokes within you. There are also "finger labyrinths," either a grooved replica of a labyrinth in wood or a simple paper copy that you trace with your finger. One practice I did—and occasionally with directees—when I lived near a historic English-style garden with various paths in Evanston, Illinois, was to treat it like a labyrinth and to walk with a question in mind to see what images or insights might be evoked.

Retreat

Setting aside time for prayer and spiritual reflection at a place dedicated to personal retreats allows for a convergence of thin time and place. Retreat centers, as well as church worship spaces, are set aside to nurture your spiritual life. I have taken personal retreats at St. Gregory's Abbey in Three Rivers, Michigan, regularly since the late 1970s. Over time I have grown closer to that men's Episcopal community in the Benedictine monastic tradition and eventually became a life-professed oblate. While serving as a parish priest at St. John's Episcopal Church, Charlotte, Michigan, I would occasionally take men on a weekend retreat either there or at a Lutheran-affiliated Benedictine priory, St. Augustine's House, in Oxford, Michigan. Women from the parish occasionally made retreats at the Hermitage in Three Rivers, a Mennonite contemplative retreat house.[14]

Taking dedicated time away from the routines of daily life by setting a day or more apart for prayer and reflection at a retreat house is an ancient spiritual practice. Monastic communities often see hospitality for retreatants as a central part of their mission, welcoming those who wish to participate in the community's hours of prayer and providing a quiet setting for reflection and prayer. In such retreat settings, the opportunity arises for thin times, when symbols emerge from the inner depths and God's wisdom to provide guidance, and when the internal spiritual process of the *via negativa*, the stripping away and letting go, occurs, preparing the way for new insight and direction.

Pilgrimage

Many major faith traditions support making spiritual journeys to sacred places rich in historical and religious significance. In 2009, my wife and I traveled to St. George's College in Jerusalem and made a pilgrimage to the "Palestine of Jesus." There we visited many holy sites in Israel and the Occupied Territories mentioned in the Gospel stories of Jesus's travels, life, ministry, crucifixion, resurrection, and postresurrection appearances.

People make pilgrimages to other holy sites—thin places and sacred destinations—making a commitment to set aside time for a journey of self-discovery and encounter with others and the Divine. Geoffrey Chaucer's fourteenth-century *Canterbury Tales* relates stories of such a ragtag group going to that spiritual center in England. Lourdes, France, is a thin place for Catholic pilgrimage associated with miraculous healing. Many have walked the pilgrimage route of the "Way of St. James" in Spain toward its destination, the Cathedral of Santiago de Compostela in Galicia.

During our sabbatical in the fall of 2013, my wife and I went on several pilgrimage journeys. We visited the Taizé Community in France, an ecumenical Christian monastic community formed gradually in the 1940s, when seven men made formal commitment to monastic community in 1949. Brother Roger Louis Schütz-Marsauche, of the Protestant Reformed tradition, provided the vision and led the effort. The community seeks to be an instrument of reconciliation within Christianity and among the poor, and the name of the current place of worship in Taizé illustrates this desire: the Church of *Reconciliation*. Currently more than one hundred brothers belong to monastic community, many living in Taizé, but some in other parts of the world living among the poor. These brothers come from both Catholic and Protestant churches, from thirty different countries, speaking multiple languages. Since the 1960s the Taizé Community has attracted tens of thousands of visitors each year, especially young people—the vast majority of visitors—who seek deepened, spiritual lives. We had known of the Taizé Community for many years, having become familiar with its chants that have made their way into worship services. We also attended various local Taizé-style ecumenical worship services that focused on chants in various languages, simple reading of Scripture, often in several languages, followed by a sustained silence with the possibility of devotion before the cross using votive candles and simple prayers.

Various symbols are present in the Church of Reconciliation, including blocks of varying sizes and shapes lit from within by votive candles, large orange banners in the form of triangular sails, and large, striking icons. The function of the symbols is left open for personal interpretation and communication with God:

> Without a doubt, Taizé is filled with symbolism. In fact, over the years different accounts have been purported as to what the various symbols mean. Note, however, that at Taizé, there is no unifying or single symbolic imagery that the brothers are attempting to employ. Each brother will find different meanings in the symbols around the church, and likewise, each pilgrim is free to interpret these symbols in their own way. This is an important aspect of Taizé. The brothers purposely use symbols with open meanings. One of the brothers explained that symbols should never be closed: "Symbols are meant to be suggestive, not prescriptive." Thus, most of the décor and sacred art in the church is left open for the pilgrim to interpret. In this way, "the Spirit can speak to us deep within our hearts."[15]

While on pilgrimage to the Isle of Iona in Scotland, we worshiped twice daily with the ecumenical Iona Community founded by the Rev. George MacLeod in 1938 in the restored thirteenth-century Benedictine abbey church. We walked amidst the ruins of the thirteenth-century Augustinian nunnery and admired the great high crosses dating back to the eighth and ninth centuries. Within the abbey church cloister and in the museum we found magnificent, intricately carved grave slabs and gravestones. Other restored structures such as the ninth-to-tenth-century St. Columba's Shrine and the twelfth-century St. Oran's Chapel give a living sense of the sacred history of the island.

One day a group of us took a guided pilgrimage of the island. Near the ferry landing is an area known as Martyrs Bay. The guide shared that this was the traditional location at which the early Benedictine monks, who owned no weapons and were committed to nonviolence, were killed by Vikings in a series of invasions beginning in 795. I found myself deeply moved, imagining such a scene and respecting the cost these monks were willing to pay as a witness to their faith and in obedience to Jesus Christ, whom they followed. The pilgrimage spot and reflection renewed my own commitment as a Christian and as an oblate representative of Benedictine spirituality to the gospel values of nonviolence, reconciliation, and peacemaking in a world often torn by violence and coercive oppression.

The Royal Road: Personal and Group Dreamwork

When making the pilgrimage to the Isle of Iona, I hoped I would get a "great" dream. What I actually dreamed was having to clear out garbage before going down into a dark tunnel; in another dream, I filled in for a friend by leading a worship service—in a church whose liturgical texts completely confused me. I disappointed some parishioners by improvising when they expected classic or traditional liturgy ("Chopin" in the dream). I yearned for an inspirational, breakthrough dream in which I might meet St. Columba. Instead, I got what I truly needed: a *via negativa* downward turn in both dreams. In the one I received the task of clearing out the trash; in the other, I received a solid dose of humility and resistance to liturgical change. My wife pointed out to me a possible dream pun in the word "Chopin," since I was assigned to a task group chopping vegetables in the kitchen in preparation for lunch and dinner, a good but mundane practice immediately following the Morning Prayer office. At any rate, the dreams probably more truly reflected the ordinary, earthy Celtic spirituality shaped by centuries of monasticism and the present Iona ecumenical community's values, than any big dream ever could. Where I hoped to "incubate" a great dream while on the holy Isle of Iona, what I received was a lot less than the inspirational and stellar material I anticipated, but also the truthful guidance that I needed.

Life is not always on the up and up. Often it is ordinary and messy and takes us down first, as indicated for me in the symbols of having to clear away the garbage and descend down a dark tunnel. I undoubtedly create a lot of my own garbage and need, periodically, to do some inner housecleaning. That "purgative way" of cleaning up often requires self-examination, naming those little sins that clutter my life, and repentance, responding with humility. St. Benedict, in the seventh chapter of the *Rule,* symbolized the way of spiritual health as a ladder, as in the story of Jacob. However, *ascending* the steps of the ladder took the monk ever *deeper* into humility. For Benedict, up is down, and down is up. Going into a dark tunnel sounds to me like an invitation from Wisdom to enter the unknown and relinquish control—embracing mystery rather than clinging to my own assumptions of what I think is the right product. The second dream also echoed the theme of relinquishing control and embracing humility. Here I faced my anxiety about what felt confusing to me and about not connecting with the expectations of those I was trying to serve. If I was filling in for or helping out a friend (Jesus?) by leading worship, I sure didn't know my way around that particular group. And yet, I offered what I could. I took my part as best I understood it in the life of that community and offered it in service to them and to God. That seemed to fit my feelings about being on this pilgrimage on Iona. And it helped open me to that place and people as both sacred and blessedly ordinary.

Dream Incubation

I just mentioned my desire to incubate a dream when I was on Iona. Let me say more about incubation. The practice of "incubating a dream" is very ancient. For example, there is the Old Testament story of the call of Samuel when he was a boy. His mother, Hannah, dedicated Samuel as a young child to live and serve in the temple with Eli the priest. One night Samuel kept hearing someone calling his name. He thought it was Eli, so he went to him. Eli suspected that God was calling Samuel, so he gave the boy instructions to say, "Speak, Lord, for your servant is listening." God again called Samuel, the boy responded as instructed and received a message—the first that the great prophet-priest would receive in his service to the Lord (1 Samuel 3). Sleeping, as Eli and Samuel did, in a dedicated holy place, provided the thin space where dreams involving divine revelations might incubate.

In ancient times, those seeking healing through the ministrations of the Greek god Asclepius also practiced dream incubation. People traveled to an Asclepian temple and slept there in hopes of receiving a dream visitation by Asclepius, often in the form of a serpent, that would either provide immediate healing or instructions.

In modern times, one way we can practice dream incubation is going to retreat centers or pilgrimages. Focusing on a particular need or concern and seeking some response from a dream or series of dreams— and if possible sleeping in a sacred space or thin place—increases the chances of the emergence of some relevant dream symbol. Numerous stories exist of breakthroughs in the sciences, technology, arts, literature, music, and other fields attributed to taking the issue or question into the sleeping state and receiving guidance from a dream symbol. "Sleeping on it" is not a bad practice. Also, praying for a dream that might provide guidance is something we can do as part of our discernment work.

Meaning and Interpretation

Dreams, like any other symbols, are subject to multiple levels of meaning and interpretation. Based on our particular life experience and framework of beliefs—as well as the shared or different experiences of the cultures we live in—we bring various meanings to a dream symbol. So dream symbols can have different meanings for the one who had the dream and for those who hear the dream. A particular interpretation or series of interpretations may or may not be meaningful for the dreamer. Do not impose any interpretation on a dreamer—telling someone else what her or his dream means. The best we can do when offering possible interpretations is to acknowledge that this is only *my* perspective. A phrase commonly used for offering an interpretation is: "If this were *my* dream, I . . ." The dreamer holds final authority for what is meaningful.

Support in Exploring Meaning

Having another person or group safely and creatively reflect with you on the possible meanings of your dream can help immensely. Spiritual directors often train to accompany people who wish to explore the possible meanings in the rich symbols of their dreams. I taught people to lead dreamwork groups in a seminary, a spiritual direction training program, a program for spiritual companionship group leaders, and in a parish. These groups primarily aim to help dreamers explore the symbols in their dreams to uncover what meaning and wisdom the dreams provide. But, in working together to uncover the possible meanings for the one who presented the dream, participants quickly discover that the dream has layers of meaning *for everyone,* thus providing a remarkably rich resource for the whole group. Because we share levels of meaning in group dreamwork, the shared social, religious, spiritual, political, organizational, cultural, national, and global levels of symbol interpretation are more easily discovered.

Here we might reflect a bit on the different ways groups may serve. In the West, we easily see the value—if we feel safe enough—of a group serving its individual members. A dreamwork group helps individual members explore the wide range of possible meanings of a dream and its symbols. The group typically provides a broader field of possible meanings than any individual working alone can discover . . . or even more than when the individual works with a spiritual director or psychotherapist. As the group assists the individual explore meaning, it can also focus on exploring the dream's meaning for the whole community. What additional wisdom might the dream and its symbols have for the group? While often a stretch for the individualistic Western mindset, the benefits can be enormous if we can imagine that some dreams "belong" to the group. On that level of interpretation we collectively discover wisdom and direction.

Communal Dreaming

I was first introduced to communal forms of dreamwork by reading Dr. Patricia Garfield's popular book *Creative Dreaming* soon after it came out in 1974. She brought attention to ancient and traditional dream-valuing cultures such as the Iroquois Nation and the Senoi tribe in Malaysia, in which meaning, wisdom, art, and practical solutions to problems emerging in dreams were shared for the common good.[16] I had been aware that many of the revelatory dreams and visions in Holy Scripture applied to a ruler, kingdom, or people rather than just to an individual person. Later I became aware of the dream collection of ordinary people in Berlin during the rise of the Nazis that journalist Charlotte Beradt compiled in her groundbreaking book, *The Third Reich of Dreams: The Nightmares of a Nation, 1933–39*. Beradt documented how the rising power of Hitler's Third Reich invaded and altered the collective unconscious of a nation. This began my own awakening to the potential of dreams for the community.

My work in spiritual direction while I was in Michigan connected me to several colleagues who were religious Sisters of St. Joseph based at the motherhouse in Nazareth, Michigan. Like many religious communities, their numbers in vowed profession were getting smaller and older, and they needed to re-vision the use of their facilities and the ways they could serve and connect to the wider world. These spiritual direction colleagues told me that, as part of their community's discernment process, some of them regularly gathered at breakfast to share their dreams from the night before, reflecting together on how the dreams might speak to their collective situation. The ones involved in this dream sharing called themselves "the Dream Team." Some of the insights gained from this regular dream sharing provided the foundation for their Transformations Spirituality Center. It is fitting to see the following quotation from Jan Phillips about the center on her website:

> Transformation originates in people who see a better way or a fairer world, people who reveal themselves, disclose their dreams, and unfold their hopes in the presence of others. And this very unfolding, this revelation of raw, unharnessed desire, this deep longing to be a force for good in the world is what inspires others to feel their own longings, to remember their own purpose, and to act, perhaps for the first time, in accordance with their inner spirit.[17]

When leading retreats and consultations for churches or organizations, I sometimes ask participants if anyone had a dream that might speak in some way to their community. Surprisingly, I often get a positive response, and someone will share their dream with the group. We then explore the possible meanings associated with the symbols in the dream and what they might mean to the organization. Sometimes we simply find that the dream encourages or expresses hope for the group. Other times it seems much more complex, bringing to awareness old experiences of pain or wounding that still need acknowledgment and attention, or giving expression to the group's fears, frustrations, hopes, and aspirations.

In my consultation with St. Clement's Episcopal Church in the Southside Chicago suburb of Harvey, one of the people being trained to help lead the parish's community-level discernment shared a fascinating, repeating dream that evolved over five years. During that time, the parish suffered multiple losses—the death of a major lay leader, the departure of several other important lay leaders, the sudden retirement of their rector of thirty years—and parishioners hadn't had good opportunities for processing their grief in a supportive community setting. I was invited to work with the parish for two years following a problematic interim and a failed situation with the priest called as rector after the long-term rector had left.

The initial dream featured a wedding ceremony, but everyone, including the bride and groom, was dressed in black. At the front of the church, as the bride and groom processed, stood a closed casket, which belonged to a lay church leader who had suddenly died. Behind the casket stood the sad, former rector, the presider at the marriage. The dreamer, who was the bride, said that for a long time she and the bridesmaids were driven to the church in a black limousine. Once at the church, they opened the casket, and the groom placed a white rose in it. She had this dream about once a week, and it shifted over time with slight variations: "My dress and my bridesmaids' dresses get lighter each time I have the dream. The last time I had the dream, everyone wore a kind of peach, which is one of my favorite colors. Now when I have the dream, the casket is almost always open." She also mentioned that in the dream the congregation didn't seem to notice the casket—only the bride, groom, and former rector see it. The ensuing discussion among the parish discernment advisory group members was electric. They quickly identified the images in the dream with the frustrated attempts to experience unity due to the unresolved grief and denial of the past.

In my time with the congregation, there had been opportunities to recognize the losses and feelings of failure that they shared. Six months later, about a week before I closed my time with them, the dreamer sent me an e-mail noting that she no longer dreams that dream regularly. The last time she did, she remembered that the color of the limousine had changed to "champagne"; she felt excited about that changed symbol. During the closure celebrating the work we had done together, and that the parish discernment advisory group would continue to do, the group shared this evolving dream with the entire community, recognizing the changes and healing.[18]

W. Gordon Lawrence developed a more formal communal dreaming method as a tool for organizational development, including in churches. His "Social Dreaming matrix" gathers together members of an organization with a "host" (facilitator) who initiates and records a session in which people's dreams are offered alongside associations with the dreams. After the matrix session concludes, the dreams and associations are examined for the hopes, fears, frustrations, achievements, desires, and so on that surfaced from the collective unconscious of the organization. These findings help in looking at the needs, aspirations, and operations of an organization or community. I used this model in dreamwork courses at Seabury-Western Theological Seminary, and my students hosted a social dreaming matrix session that they opened to the seminary community.

One dream that I had while teaching the practicum-style course, which included practicing social dreaming matrix sessions, serves as an example of how a dream can speak to an immediate group situation.

Ice Fishing on Soft Ice (April 1, 2003)

A group of us—some are family members and others are my students—are in a wilderness area like the Boundary Waters

Canoe Area Wilderness in Minnesota. We are near our boat but are getting ready to go ice fishing. The ice is soft with some open patches. Nice fish are jumping in the patches of open water. It takes a little effort to open up the ice with augurs and ice spoons. We all have a lifeline available to us for safety. We anticipate good fishing.

I had this dream the night before the second class practice for a social dreaming matrix session, so I offered it as the first dream we explored in that session. A number of associations emerged that related to our feelings about the course: first, exploring the boundaries and wilderness of our collective unconscious together was exciting; second, the movement into the unconscious realm can be rich and abundant but can also be dangerous; and, finally, a question about the trustworthiness of leadership, as expressed in relation to the seminary and our group, was deemed understandable. The dream also generated associations to other dreams that were then shared in the matrix session, some of which further developed the same themes.[19]

I also used the dream matrix as a discernment tool when spiritual direction colleagues and I considered opening a spirituality center in the Chicago area.[20] Two dreams were offered in the matrix session. One was of a pioneering effort to build a new cabin but still needing to convince others that the energy poured into creativity was worth the effort. Another member offered a dream that featured a wild and energetic roller-coaster ride. In the associations and debriefing following the session, important questions surfaced about how much energy it would require to set up this center and whether leaders were able to make that commitment at that time.

Shared Dream Reality

Further possibilities in communal dreaming are still in the early stages of understanding, at least according to modern Western approaches. In one terrifying dream, I encountered an overwhelming evil presence in my house. When I awoke with a start from the dream, my (former) wife was asleep beside me but clearly in distress while sleeping. I woke her up.

This chapter has offered a wide range of practices for your consideration. Which practices have you used in the past? Are there helpful practices that were not mentioned? How have the practices you have used brought insight or new understanding to a situation or to your relationship to God?

Which practices are you most drawn to? What does that say to you about your spiritual life and the way God interacts with you?

Are there practices you want to avoid or tend to discount? What do you think is behind your restrictions? Could this be a growing edge for you to explore, or does this reflect the particular

She told me she was dreaming that a powerful evil spirit was pursuing her. Both of us felt stunned at having such synchronous dreams with similar themes, taking place in the same location. It seemed to point to a shared dream reality. These dreams were pivotal in bringing us back to Christianity.

An area of dream research now underway is "mutual dreaming" or "group dreaming." Early evidence suggests that members of a dream group can have dreams that connect with other members' waking lives, or they have dreams in which they appear in each other's dreams even if they are separated by long distances or only know each other via the Internet. One organization of group dreamers dreams together for a peaceful future.[21]

In 1899 Sigmund Freud stated that dreams are the royal road to the unconscious. With the further contributions of Carl Jung, that royal road expanded from a simple analysis of manifest and latent expression of wish fulfillment to a vast arena of potential meaning. Ancient prophetic dreamers in Holy Scripture and the knowledge gained from cultural anthropologists about traditional dream-valuing societies further enrich dreams' potential as a source of creativity and wisdom, and as a guide to health, wholeness, and integration on multiple levels. These levels range from the personal, to the way we interact in our relationships, to shared societal and global concerns. Attending to our personal dreams and the dreams of our communities can provide us with significant spiritual meaning and aid in discerning God's desires.

The Book of Common Prayer service of Compline (meaning the completion of the day) offers this antiphon near the end:

> Guide us waking, O Lord, and guard us sleeping; that awake we may watch with Christ, and asleep we may rest in peace.[22]

It is a lovely part of the prayer in preparation for sleep. However, in my personal devotional prayer before sleep, I have over the years prayed a slightly modified version:

> Guide us waking, O Lord,
> and guide us sleeping;
> that awake we may watch with Christ,
> and asleep we may dream your dreams.

range of abilities and capacities you have (and don't have)? Could this be a growing edge for you to explore, or does this reflect the particular range of abilities and capacities you have (and don't have)?

The next chapter focuses on particular contexts for symbol guidance and discernment, but in considering the range of practices introduced in this chapter, which do you think would be helpful in situations involving your group (couples, family, and community) deliberations?

Would the practices need to be modified? How would you introduce such practices to your group?

4 Contexts for Discernment and Guiding Symbols

GUIDING SYMBOLS EMERGE to serve our deepest aspirations and vocational direction, supporting our well-being as we move toward greater wholeness and participate in God's mission, compassion, unity, and shalom. In this chapter I provide topical examples of the emergence of guiding symbols in personal situations, in the context of family or life partnership, in community or organizational discernment, and in societal and global issues.

Personal Direction

Finding our way in life is a deeply personal but rarely individual matter. I offer the following examples of situations and symbols for potential spiritual discernment arising from my own life. In my early years, I often tried to make sense of things on my own, although my parents and other family members offered guidance. In my adolescent years, I opened more to friends; we were often "the blind leading the blind." Only after returning to my Christian community and its resources did I also begin benefiting from spiritual directors and spiritual-companionship groups in reflecting on meaning and direction.

Symbols of a "Real Man"

I grew up when the image of a "real" man was that of the silent, rugged, individualistic, Marlboro Man–type who rarely expressed himself except in anger, competition, or sexual want—with a cigarette and alcoholic drink readily at hand: not a very healthy symbol for mature masculinity. That isolated and constricted symbol of a man, thankfully, underwent a slow, social transformation.

I like to share a story about a road trip with my cousin when we were teenagers. Greg and I have always been close cousins. We lived at great distance from each other, so we eagerly anticipated the chance to get together. In the summer of my sixteenth year I rode the bus down to Decatur, Georgia, where Greg was then living. Since both of us had driver's licenses, we asked his parents if we could take their Volkswagen Beetle for a weekend camping trip to Hartwell Dam, a beautiful reservoir on the boundary of Georgia and South Carolina. To our great surprise, they gave us approval to make the journey.

As we packed up the food and fishing and camping gear into the tiny car, we considered what would be manly things to take with us on the camping trip. It would be really great to have women companions, but a *Playboy* magazine would have to do. Real men would also have beer with them. Finally, men would have cigarettes. Beer was going to have to wait, since we were underage and didn't know anyone who would buy for us. That still left us with cigarettes and a *Playboy* magazine.

Into the car we went and started our journey: seeking to do the things that men do, and thereby becoming men. It did not take long to muster up the courage to get a pack of cigarettes. We both had enjoyed the Newport commercials on television, so we thought we'd give them a try. The commercials often evoked images of mountains, lakes, and fresh spring air elicited by lighting a match and sucking on mentholated tobacco. I think we used a cigarette coin vendor, guarding against any busybody that might question our age. We were approaching the Tobacco Belt, and there were plenty of opportunities to get cigarettes.

Getting a *Playboy* magazine was more problematic. We went drugstore to drugstore, town to town, searching for the magazine with the nude centerfold. Finally, we asked a merchant if there were any *Playboy* magazines available. His reply was, "Sorry, boys, but we don't carry that kind of magazine in these here parts." We then realized that, although we were in the Tobacco Belt, we were also in the Bible Belt, and the standard of public decency and morality was upheld by banning *Playboy* magazine. We had traveled 150 miles in a futile search for a centerfold. So much for booze and sex.

We finally made it to Hartwell Dam and set up camp. It was a beautiful setting. I did most of the fishing, Greg never having really enjoyed the sport. We both tried Newport mentholated cigarettes. Greg quit for good after the first puff or so. I sucked them down and continued to abuse my lungs with tobacco for the next twenty-four years.

I look back with a mixture of wonder and humor on those days of relative innocence, thinking of the curious cultural symbols we inherited of mature manhood: the three forbidden fruits of soft-core pornography, alcohol, and tobacco. We were vulnerable to marketing and to our macho culture to describe our masculinity. It took many more years for me to embrace the deeper dimensions of mature masculinity—being a creative and productive person of vocation, giving and receiving gifts in an interdependent relationship with my community, being a loving and nurturing husband and father, growing in my own physical, emotional, social, and spiritual well-being, and supporting that same growth in those God gives to me in my relationships. Sadly, relatively few men in our society can give effective witness to a deeper view of mature manhood. They are present and available, however, if young men are willing to look and the older men are willing to mentor.[1]

Warnings, Hopes, and Aspirations

When I was seventeen years old, I confided to my Grandpa Lyon, a retired Christian Church (Disciples of Christ) minister, that I thought God was calling me to ordained ministry. I was leader of the youth group at church and had been invited to preach a sermon. Many of my uncles were ordained ministers. It seemed like a reasonable choice of profession, and one to which I felt attracted. He wisely counseled me that if the calling were from God, then eventually I would answer the call and become a minister, but for the present time not to give it too much thought. That advice freed me to be the young man I was, allowing for questioning and exploration as I readied myself for college, not forcing or hurrying the process.

Culturally, my college years were a turbulent time. The civil rights movement became increasingly violent in the aftermath of Martin Luther King Jr.'s assassination. The Vietnam War escalated, as did antiwar protests and demonstrations of civil disobedience. I helped organize antiwar demonstrations and political debates at my community college, then affiliated with the radical Students for a Democratic Society (SDS) at my university and joined in antiwar demonstrations in that locale.

Eastern religions grew in popularity, as did free speech, "drugs, sex, and rock 'n' roll," and a deep distrust of institutions—social, political, economic, and religious. I began practicing Eastern-style meditation and soon was also experimenting with drugs. At the age of twenty, I dropped out of college for a year to force a review of my draft status so I could seek reclassification as a conscientious objector (which was granted); I also got married. My poor parents—a minister's daughter and an adoptive father, a retired military officer working for the defense department—endured much from me at that time.

And yet, I was also on a vital spiritual journey. One night when I was nineteen years old, I was surprised by a unitive experience: I was caught up in a divine cosmic dance. I was drug- and alcohol-free when this event occurred, and it was as intense and consciousness-bending as any "peak experience" that Abraham Maslow might have described. My journal notes read:

Cosmic Dance (c. 1967)

I went with a friend of mine to a little camping trailer, owned by his parents, for an overnight outing. The trailer was set in a field near a river outside of Union City, Michigan. It was nighttime, and I told Jim that I was going to go outside for a little while. Oh, what a beautiful night it was! It was a clear, starry night. The river started making music—it truly did. [I later wrote a poem about that night, but I lost it. A fragment I still remember: "Water is rushing past rocks / And the melody rings with the sound . . ."] I became intoxicated with the music of the river. The ground began vibrating to the rhythm of the river. The diamond-bright stars began moving. I was caught up in the dance. And I danced with the cosmos, and I was danced by something wonderful and mysterious beyond me.

This invitation to the divine dance, both frightening in its intensity and wonderful for being caught up in some Mystery, overwhelmed me. The experience was beautiful, grand, and very much beyond me and my puny capacity for control. I didn't think I had gone crazy, but I wasn't sure; I believed the moment was somehow connected with spiritual experiences I had read about in Eastern spiritual writing. But, in my Baptist Church experience, I had no I clear religious frame of reference to draw upon. I tried describing to my parents what had happened to me, and they suggested I talk to my pastor. I set up an appointment with my pastor and sought his guidance. Although he was a compassionate listener, he also seemed completely baffled by any kind of mystical experience and gave me no help in understanding what had happened or what to do about it. And so I launched myself on a spiritual search for understanding that took me at times to dark practices and a lot of drug abuse and chemical dependency as I attempted to go beyond normal states of consciousness.

This began the period of dreams that I was in a classroom and had to take a test but—to my great discomfort—realized I had been studying the wrong subjects and was totally unprepared. At that time, I was without a spiritual guide, and, while aware of the implications of the dreams, I was also ignorant of what Christian mystical theology and spirituality might hold for me. The Christian faith I then knew felt sterile, confining, doctrinally rigid, skeptical of anything related to mysticism, and lacking in meaningful engagement with the important social and political issues of the times. I was aware of what no longer fit my understanding of Christianity, and I yearned for a more direct relationship with the Divine than what was possible in the spiritual life I had known.

Although for a decade I advanced in my career, working for and being promoted in the Michigan Department of Social Services, my spiritual and emotional health deteriorated. A year and one day before I had the terrifying dream of the powerful evil presence that brought me to plead for Christ's protection, I had a liberating, numinous dream that gave me hope amidst my growing depression, isolation, and aimlessness.

Beauty of the God-Seekers (April 29, 1977)

I awaken [a false awakening] and find myself on a bunk bed in a dormitory room in Alcatraz Prison. I get up and leave the room while others sleep. The whole place is dark and dismal. I feel desolate and begin wandering aimlessly. I come to a large, dimly lit auditorium and see a woman standing by a lectern, which is illuminated. This woman is tall and dressed in a white robe. There is a sense of majesty about her—a numinous quality that does not seem entirely human. I move closer to her and see that she is reading from a large book. She says aloud, "May the beauty of the God-seekers be with you." Then she turns to me and adds, "This is for you."

I feel empowered by those words. I see a stairway, and I climb up to a loft. There is a window open to the night sky. I remember the words and, with a yell that comes from deep within me, I leap out the window and fly free.

That sentence, "May the beauty of the God-seekers be with you," became a benediction for me. It affirmed my spiritual quest, even in darkness when I could not see where my journey led.

Spiritual Warfare

The dream about being freed from (my inner) prison expressed my deep spiritual hope for liberation, but my life continued to deteriorate for another year. I had learned over ten years that there was a spiritual realm and had explored parts of it, but my exploration remained unguided, with no reliable map or counsel about what forces might inhabit this realm. My feelings of isolation and depression deepened over the year, and I looked for some way to make a change from what I knew. At that time, the Bible prophecy book by Hal Lindsey, *The Late Great Planet Earth*, had gained popularity and was recommended by a Christian neighbor.[2] I read it and was fascinated by the apocalyptic symbolism drawn from the Bible and the urgency of the interpretation that the evangelist conveyed to his audience. I believed in the spiritual realm and the powerful spiritual forces at work in the world. These forces felt palpable and threatened to break through in me and in the world. Maybe Christianity and the Bible had something important to say about this, something I had missed in my previous study. I talked about this with my (then) wife, Colleen. Then I had a powerful dream, *as did my wife*:

The Decision (April 30, 1978)

I was in the kitchen and saw a book that looked like the lost Bible my Grandpa Lyon had given me when I was baptized. I said to my wife that I had found my Bible and started looking at it. The book came apart in the center, and there was *another* bound book. I looked at a chapter in the first book, and the chapter was titled differently than the Bible. I then looked at the other book. Some of the passages were in an unknown language. Other passages, in English, were about sorcery and black magic. It was an occult text like the Necronomicon,[3] and I sensed that the power that I had sought in dark arts was now available to me. I then had an oppressive feeling of a powerful evil presence nearby. In a panic I started fumbling through the other book and saw a full-color picture. The picture showed two roads—one leading to Christ and another leading to Satan. I then feared that the devil was trying to capture my soul and was far more powerful than I was. I said aloud that I believed in the power of God to overcome evil and that Jesus would save me, and I pleaded for that help. I then had a feeling that this was a "breakthrough dream" and woke my wife up. [This was a false awakening, but I then heard my wife moan, and I woke her up.] She related to me her dream, in which a powerful and evil spirit had pursued her from the garage to the house; she had been terrified and was calling for my help.

Through those dream encounters I began to realize on a gut level that a malignant, autonomous, intelligent, and invasive evil exists in the universe. My wife and I had opened ourselves to this evil over time, and now we could see through our dream encounters that it had drawn near. We felt the terror of recognizing this evil as beyond our capacity to control or defend against. In my dream, I recognized that I needed nothing less than divine intervention. Without Christ's help, I was afraid that I would lose my humanity, that the quest for personal power I had begun years before opened me to evil.

The morning following these synchronous breakthrough dreams, my wife and I attended an Episcopal Church, where we eventually became members. Communion that morning was unexpectedly powerful for me. A few hours earlier we had had our synchronous dreams; shortly after, in accepting the sacramental bread and wine, I felt an overwhelming sense of Presence, lightness of body and spirit, peace, and strength.

As we continued to attend that church, I discovered that the faith community had entrusted me with a greater sense of personal freedom than had previous churches. An environment of spiritual hospitality freed me to explore the Christian faith, raise questions and doubts, and find respect.

I also discovered a treasury of Christian spiritual and mystical literature that covered the entire history of Christianity, rather than just post-Reformation literature. The books of Morton Kelsey proved crucial to my struggle to make sense of the spiritual reality I had experienced and now needed to understand in light of Jungian psychology and Christian spirituality.

But my newfound encounter with the Christian faith and spiritual life as an adult approaching age thirty was also difficult, a turbulent time of reorientation, a liminal time when I struggled to let go of unhealthy behaviors and spiritual beliefs. I worked hard to test out and take on my new life. A group in the church helped guide me as I went through these changes. Not surprisingly, I experienced a number of intense dreams that mirrored this turbulence and my desire for change. One lucid dream in particular, which felt like spiritual warfare, spoke deeply to me of my desire to know God and to be faithful amidst the spiritual challenges I faced.

Diamond Room (August 8, 1978)

My family is gathered at night in beds in an unfamiliar setting. They lead me downstairs to an old grandfather clock and yell, "Surprise! This is your birthday present!" and then start singing the Happy Birthday song. I realize this isn't my birthday and that it must be a dream. I should seek my God.

It's still dark, but now I'm in an old, dimly lit castle with a sword in my hand. Suddenly I'm attacked by men with swords. I think: This is strange. I seek God, and instead I'm attacked by demons. I'll have to rely on the Holy Spirit to guide my sword just to get out alive. I lash at the opponents and kill one after the other, but each foe is progressively more skilled. I think that I may have to fight Satan himself. Then a powerful warrior confronts me from about twenty yards away. He has a sword much shorter than mine, but he throws it at me and barely misses. He has other short swords, and I realize with dismay that he is skilled at sword throwing. He sends a barrage at me through the air. They whistle past my head, and I hide behind a pillar.

Other demons are coming nearer. I get one of the swords that the warrior had thrown at me and ineffectively throw it back at him. A demon with a trident nearly hits me from the side, but I kill him, grab the spear, and throw it at the sword-thrower. I hit him, and he falls. I hear others yell, "Get him before he reaches the Diamond Room."

After fighting several more "men," I get to a room with a golden hue. There are several men there, absolutely beautiful, powerful beings. I attack one, and he defends himself, but my sword strikes him in his middle. He doesn't fall, and there is no wound. I strike him several times and realize that he is immortal—an angel—and that the Diamond Room is God's own throne room! I remember that, in Revelation, John saw God as like a living gem. I feel overwhelmed by the knowledge that I am in the presence of God and fall on my knees.

There is much to see in the symbols of this dream. Most meaningful to me was the need to rely on the Holy Spirit to guide me in the battle with my demonic attackers (my own inner demons). I felt sheer wonder in the presence of the angelic beings serving in the throne room of God. The knowledge that I was in the presence of the Divine brought me to my knees in worship. I am reminded of Rudolph Otto who, in *The Idea of the Holy*, wrote of the psychological experience of numinous encounters. He observed that the human often feels their "creatureliness" in the face of the Divine, a sense of fascination, and an overwhelming sense of the *mysterium tremendum* (awe, fear, and trembling in the face of such a tremendous mystery).

I continue to affirm the wisdom of relying on the Holy Spirit. I know that we will always battle our inner demons and temptations. But I no longer have the desire to destroy them as much as to, with God's grace, convert or integrate those energies into service for the realm of God and our wholeness. I now tend to see the vices or demons as virtues or energies that have gone astray, needing healthy boundaries and the healing spirit of Christ to bring them into right alignment. We cannot do this work without divine grace, and there are no assurances that we will be successful in the short run. Nor, as I have remarked about "The Decision" dream (p. 115), do I always believe that evil is just a distortion of the good. I am now more confident—through God's unconditional love—that we have access to that inner mansion, castle, or throne room where God has always dwelled within us.

Fire!

The symbol of fire has often been used to describe the spiritual life. God called to Moses out of the burning bush, calling him to lead Israel from slavery in Egypt to become a people in covenant with God. In the Exodus experience, God leads Israel in the desert by a pillar of fire by night and a cloud by day. Various Scripture passages, using the metaphor of the refiner's fire, refer to our spiritual lives being tested and purified. John the Baptist looks to the one who comes after him as baptizing with the Holy Spirit and fire (Matt. 3:11). In the story of Pentecost in Acts 2, what appeared to be tongues of fire rested on the heads of Jesus's followers.

One of my favorite sayings of the desert elders is this:

> Abba Lot came to Abba Joseph and said: Father, according as
> I am able, I keep my little rule, and my little fast, my prayer,
> meditation and contemplative silence; and according as I am
> able I strive to cleanse my heart of thoughts: now what more
> should I do? The elder rose up in reply and stretched out his
> hands to heaven, and his fingers became like ten lamps of
> fire. He said: Why not be totally changed into fire?[4]

Early in my adult Christian spiritual journey, I spent a night in
prayer and meditation, seeking an anointing of the Holy Spirit. I vowed
that I would go the entire night in vigil if I needed to. When dawn finally came, I was exhausted and disappointed, feeling like I had failed
to receive God's blessing. I fell asleep. Several hours later I awoke from
this dream:

Being Fire! (ca. 1978–1979)

I am burning, covered and filled with fire, but I am not being
consumed or harmed. I am enflamed by a holy fire.

Similarly, in the summer following my second year of seminary, I
recorded this lucid dream:

Flame (June 26, 1983)

I am with a friend and am wearing shorts, and then see that I
am wearing jeans—a sign that I was dreaming.

I wished to focus on seeking God and find that I am float-
ing bodily in the air. I am in a congregation gathered for Holy
Eucharist, and I float up to the altar's Eucharistic candles. First
I entered and went into and up the flame on the right candle,
and then I did the same with the left candle. The flame did
not hurt me—I, too, was flame.

Both of these dreams express the spiritual aspiration of being "on fire" with a passionate devotion to God, reminiscent of John of the Cross's mystical poem "Living Flame of Love," whose first stanza reads:

> O living flame of love
> whose tender burning fire
> wounds sore my soul within its deepest center!
> No more depriving of
> completing your desire,
> now burst the veil, perfect this sweet encounter![5]

Answer to a Bureaucrat's Prayer

In the latter part of 1978, I became increasingly restless with my work at the Michigan Department of Social Services and felt more drawn to ordained ministry in the Episcopal Church. Several people in the congregation suggested that I consider this possibility, and it awakened my old sense of vocational call that I mentioned to my grandfather when I was seventeen and had carried with me into my first years of college.

When I turned thirty in September 1978, my mother gave me a box of clipped newspaper articles on my debate achievements in high school, church youth leadership, Eagle Scout recognition, and so on—scrapbook stuff. I received the box and put it aside. During that time, I felt such inner turmoil about whether this was the time to begin being considered for ordained ministry that I said a prayer: "God, if this is a call from you to let go of my career and become a priest, I want to see it in black and white, otherwise please get off my back. This inner struggle is becoming too much for me. Amen." For several months I experienced peace and quiet, able to focus again at work.

But then the turmoil returned . . . forcefully. The interior unrest and sense that "now is the time" grew so strong that one night I opened the box my mom had given me and started randomly going through it as a distraction from the distress. I came upon a single-spaced, typewritten letter several pages long that my Uncle Don had sent to me while he was in seminary and I was ten years old. It began by saying that it would not be long before I was all grown up, and, although I then wanted to be a doctor, he suggested that I consider becoming a "doctor of the soul" and go into the ordained ministry. He continued for several pages about his understanding of ordained ministry and why I should consider it. I couldn't remember having read this letter before, and I felt stunned. I believed God had met the impossible "put-it-in-black-and-white" demand of my bureaucratic prayer. I then began the initial steps to ordained ministry in my church.

A Grandfather's Blessing

Twice when I was at the point of major vocational change, I dreamed of my late grandfather, the Rev. C. B. Lyon. The first time this happened I was about to leave my job with social services to start seminary. In the dream, my grandfather and I attend the same party. When I see him, I say that it is wonderful to see him again, "even though you are dead." He smiles, and it felt like he was watching over me and blessing me as I began this major step on my vocational journey.

I don't recall any details of the second dream, except that again I felt that I had my grandfather's blessing as a minister. At that time, I was about to leave my work after eleven years as a parish priest and rector of St. John's Episcopal Church in Charlotte, Michigan, following my wife Ruth's beginning as a full-time teacher at Seabury-Western Theological Seminary (now Bexley Seabury) in the fall of 1995. It was again a time of major vocational change, since I had, for the previous two years, been offering spiritual direction and formation programs on a part-time basis. I was now launching that ministry full-time as Lamb & Lion Spiritual Guidance Ministries.

Both of those dedicated shifts in direction resulted from serious spiritual discernment that had involved deliberations with others. Those influenced by Ignatian discernment principles sometimes use the language of "looking for a sign of confirmation" when they have arrived at a tentative decision and then seek a sign that the direction has been affirmed by God. In both of those situations, I had received the affirmation of others about the direction I was about to take, but the dreams of my grandfather gave me the internal symbolic affirmation that strengthened my resolve to make these changes.

Completing a Transition

In August 2009, Ruth and I moved from Evanston, Illinois, to the San Francisco Bay area after she accepted a teaching position in Berkeley at Church Divinity School of the Pacific. This was a big move for us across country. A Midwesterner all my life, for more than sixty years, I was entering a new world out West. I felt anxious about the change but also excited about exploring this new world and expecting that it would work out all right. Five months into living in California, I had a dream that reflected, with a big dash of humor, the continuing anxiety of this major life transition.

If You Can't Escape the Bear. . . (January 15, 2010)

I am with some other men in a large cabin. A big brown bear comes up and tries to get in. I warn the others about the bear. It finally breaks through the wall, and we scatter to escape. I go out the back door and down a large hill and hide behind a big log near the water's edge of a lake. I look for a weapon but can only find a branch of wood that crumbles in my hand.

I move away from the area and soon come up to a small settlement. I see the bear coming again. I go into a tavern and yell that there's a bear coming! The bear comes up to me at a table and sits down. I see a couple of green beans on the table and offer him one. He's not interested but wants to hang out with me. He orders a scotch "Slurpee" from the bartender, and the bartender gives him a big mug of scotch blended with ice. I ask the bear what the scotch is, and he says it's Ballantine's. I think that is a fairly cheap grade of scotch, but this is a bear after all and may not have very refined taste. I decide to join him by ordering a Ballantine's Slurpee for myself.

I awoke laughing. And I wondered about that brown bear and what it might represent. A brown bear is a grizzly, and they were hunted out of existence in California in the early 1920s. Although I had treated the dream bear as a threat, it kept pursuing me in order to offer friendship. I kept the dream-bear symbol in my mind as I went on with the day. Later that day I saw my bear and again had to laugh. Predominant on the "California Republic" state flag is the image of a grizzly bear. I then began to feel truly welcomed by this wild and wonderful state and started making it my new home. To celebrate my dream friendship with the California bear, I bought a bottle of Ballantine's scotch and enjoyed it "on the rocks" rather than as a "Slurpee."

Getting Ready for a Change

You have read in this section some of my own stories and dreams about seeking personal spiritual discernment, and how dreams or other symbols have illuminated my way. Sometimes they warned me. Sometimes they challenged my outlook. Sometimes they supported a movement in my life. Sometimes they helped me see more clearly. After I came into the Episcopal Church, I began regular reflection with others, including spiritual directors, to help me understand situations as occasions for spiritual discernment. I was also becoming equipped to guide others in their own discernment process.

In my practice as a spiritual director as well as a priest in parish ministry, I have helped others look at their lives and face major transitions with the tools of spiritual discernment. I have already mentioned how the symbol of a barren field evolved over time for a directee who had retired and was exploring life, having let go of her ongoing professional commitments as a parish priest. That evolving symbol became a source of hope for her that life continued to develop and that God's creative and providential care could be trusted.

> Where did you find the greatest connections between the stories of personal direction in this section and your own life? Were there stories that you felt uneasy with?

Another ordained minister for whom I served as spiritual director was early in his career when we began meeting. He had worked as associate rector in a church for several years and enjoyed many benefits in that position. However, as time moved on, he began noticing an internal shift in his interests. He pictured his work situation as a warm and cozy nest and himself as a baby eagle. But as time passed, he felt he had grown bigger and so had started peeking at the world outside the nest. At that time, he had initiated the search for a call to serve as a rector of a church. Eventually he felt like he could fly on his own and was ready to leave the nest. A position as rector of a church opened up that looked like a good fit for his abilities and interests. He accepted the position. Just as the symbols of fallow ground and mysterious seeds had provided guidance for a retired person to live into her future, so too the symbols of a growing eagle struggling to leave its secure nest helped prepare another directee for his future call.

Questions for Individual Discernment

Use these additional questions as you consider your own spiritual journey:

- What events or situations do you value in telling the story of your spiritual life?
- If you could give a title, such as the title for a book chapter, or picture an image for each major movement in your life, what would they be?
- Did particular guiding symbols emerge from those situations or events that helped clarify your direction? If so, how did you access those symbols?
- Are there situations you are now discerning? Can you locate where you are in the "spiritual discernment cycle"? Are you engaging in practices for cultivating guiding symbols?
- Who is assisting you—or who would you would like to assist you—in your discernment?

Couples and Family

In our relationships as couples and families, we face many decisions that call us to explore our hopes, values, faith, fears, yearnings, and needs. Important questions arise, such as:

- Is our relationship moving to a place of greater commitment?

▸ How do we handle career and vocational goals between us?

▸ How does the way we manage our finances express our sense of stewardship of God's resources?

▸ How do we pray about the decisions that face us?

▸ How do we decide if this is the time to start a family?

▸ What concerns or hopes do we have for our children?

▸ What is needed in caring for aging parents?

Sometimes the reflection and discernment on such questions occurs between partners alone, but often other people can assist in exploring issues and reflecting on how God might be involved. Spiritual directors, facilitated small groups, family or couples counseling, church community relationships, conversations with a pastor, friends and elder family members can all play a supportive role in deliberations. In this section, I share examples of symbols that help direction with couples and families, as well as tools for bringing guiding symbols to conscious awareness.

Symbols on the Prayer-Room Table

My wife and I have had a "prayer room" in both our houses, dedicated space for us to share a short version of Morning Prayer and other prayer or deep reflection. The room also provides a place for me to meet in direction sessions with my spiritual companions. For many years now, we have kept several objects on a table that serve as symbolic reminders of God's presence and of our desire to be present to each other and God. These symbols also remind me of my vocation as a spiritual guide and a person of prayer and discernment.

> Take a tour of your household. What things stand out as primary symbols for your shared life and values?

One such object is an oil lamp, which we light for our prayer times and for my spiritual direction sessions with clients. For me, lighting the lamp is a prayer asking for God's wisdom and light to illuminate us and the situations and concerns we bring to a prayer or direction session. The warm light reminds me that God's grace and presence give light to our paths. Even in the darkest nights of our lives, the light of God's love still shines and will not be overcome.

A ceramic statue of a lion and a lamb lying together also resides on the table. Many years ago, someone who had worked at a church I served learned that I had named my ministry Lamb & Lion Spiritual Guidance Ministries and thought the statue would be appropriate. I based the name loosely on the Isaiah 11 passage imagining the peaceable kingdom where God's shalom reigns. The name also alludes to Revelation 5, in which Jesus is called both "the Lion of the tribe of Judah" and "the Lamb." My mission is to provide spiritual opportunities to integrate both sides of ourselves—the gentle and the fierce—with God's grace for new health, wholeness, and peace within ourselves, in interpersonal relationships, and in society and the world.

If each of you in the partnership were symbolized by an animal, what would it be? Is there mutual agreement on this?

A third object lives on our table: a wood carving of a monk that my brother Hans gave to me. I see the little monk as my alter ego—I am, after all, a Benedictine oblate attached to a monastery. A retired abbot of a monastery used to tell visitors at his abbey, "Inside everyone there is a little monk." Indeed, the monk or nun may well be an archetypal figure for that part of us all that yearns for union with the Holy One and that is dedicated to practices that draw us into the sacred. I love that little monk on my table. I like to position him facing the light of the oil lamp. He looks to me to have a rather dull but quizzical expression on his face, and he is scratching his head . . . trying to figure out this incredible holy mystery. Sometimes I show him to others on retreats or as part of presentations. Once someone suggested that he isn't dumb, he's using his cell phone—talking to God. So, as you can see, symbols do produce multiple meanings.

Occasionally our table holds a stone or two. We both appreciate the good Earth, and we reverence the creation that God made and pronounced "very good" (Gen. 1:31). Holding on to a stone can be a tactile prayer of solidity and earthy spirituality. In Scripture, a rock also symbolizes strength and protection. During turmoil in the lives of my loved ones, my prayer image became one of crawling up on a large rock amidst the powerful, roiling river sweeping around me and threatening to pull me into its currents. Sometimes one of my loved ones would appear in the prayer; I would hold out a hand to help them onto the rock with me. Over months, the prayer image shifted. As our collective emotional situation changed, the rock grew into a verdant and pleasant land that I could enjoy.

Now Is the Time

On several occasions, I looked for some confirming symbol that the time was right for a major action related to my relationship with Ruth. One such occasion arose when deciding when to propose to her. In a journal entry for September 1988, I write about a dream in which Ruth wore a ring. This prompted me to purchase an engagement ring and propose to her within a week.

After two years of marriage, we started talking about adopting a child. At first I was resistant to taking on such a responsibility, since I already had a child from my previous marriage and had been a custodial single parent for nine years. I felt unsure about our having the energy to care for a new child while also working in our respective ministries. I also knew, however, that Ruth yearned for a child, and I took her desires to heart. I then dreamed about a little boy for whom I felt tenderly: he was my son! I decided I was willing and ready to start the adoption process. Eventually we did adopt a ten-year-old boy as our son. When I first saw him, I believed I had seen him before in my dream.

In the Same Boat Together

As a church pastor, I was sometimes called upon to provide guidance and support when parishioners faced rocky situations in their marriages. On occasion, I offered a guided-imagery meditation based Mark 4's story of Jesus stilling the storm. In the story, the disciples ride in a boat when a great windstorm arises, sending up waves that threaten to swamp them. Jesus sleeps on a cushion in the stern of the boat. The disciples cry out to him to awaken. "Don't you care if we perish?" they ask. Jesus calls for the wind and the sea to "Be still!" Calm settles on the water, and the disciples wonder, "Who *is* this man who commands the wind and sea?"

Jesus Calming the Storm

I ask the couple (or individual) to imagine themselves on the boat together and, if appropriate, with other family members:

1. Imagine a storm is brewing, threatening everyone.
   ▸ What is the storm like?
2. Experience the wind, the waves, the violent rocking of the boat.
   ▸ How do you feel?
   ▸ What do you say to the others in the boat?
3. Now imagine calling Jesus to the scene.
   ▸ What do you ask him?
   ▸ What does he say to you about what will calm your storm?

4. If you have questions for Jesus about any of this, ask him.

5. Finally, imagine the sea calming and the boat coming to a safe harbor.

After the meditation, I invite the meditator(s) to debrief:

▸ What was your experience in the meditation?

▸ What wisdom from the meditation applies to your situation?

Ignatian-Style Disadvantages and Advantages

A set of discernment considerations, drawn from methods that go back to the deliberations by Ignatius and his companions, can be useful for couples, families, and communities. I introduced this method in step three of the spiritual discernment cycle (p. 32). The goal is to spend an equal amount of time with advantages and disadvantages around a particular issue, while attending to images or feeling that arise in each category. My wife and I used this method while in discernment about a possible job for her. During a retreat our daily categories for thought, meditation, and prayer were:

1. The disadvantages if Ruth accepts the job if it is offered to her.
2. The disadvantages if she does not accept the job and we remain in our current situation.
3. The advantages if Ruth accepts the job if it is offered to her.
4. The advantages if Ruth does not accept the job and we remain in our current situation.

Do not just make the lists as if creating a balance sheet and tallying it up. Pay attention to what kind of "energy" or "affect" (feeling) is present as you address each category. What images or symbols emerge that provide guidance? Where do these images take us in our relationship to each other and to God? I described (on p. 32) how an image and feeling of freedom arose from one of my Tai Chi (Qigong) exercises while spending a day considering one of the categories. At another time during the retreat, I had a prayer vision of Jesus assuring me that, in either choice, he would be with us and could make our work prosper. These visions, too, were vital to the direction of the discernment.

Quaker-Style Clearness Committee

In the Quaker tradition, individuals and couples can draw upon the resources of a prayerful community to assist them in their discernment. The "clearness committee"—essentially a small group invited by the discerners and led by a facilitator ("clerk" in the Quaker terminology)—assists the ones seeking discernment. Discerners may prepare a preliminary written statement about the situation they are facing ("Are we called to be married?" "Do we make this move?" etc.) and what they have already considered. A clearness committee believes that God has already placed the truth or direction on the discerners' hearts and that its task is to provide ample silence, prayer, and evocative questions to help the discerners clear away the clouds to discover their truth. After the discerners describe their situation and where they currently are in considering direction, the committee asks questions borne out of the deep, prayerful silence in which all are immersed.[6] Sometimes an image emerges for the discerner(s) or a committee member in response to a question or from the silent prayer. They then share and explore the symbol as part of the discernment session.

Family Practices

Praying and sharing images. It may seem obvious but is worth noting: We can *pray together* as a couple or as a family about the important matters for which we seek God's guidance and direction. This is easier if the couple or family already prays together each day. In addition, if an image does emerge for someone—in a dream or while meditating—it can be offered to the others for their consideration. As with the Sisters of St. Joseph's "Dream Team" or the Senoi pattern of family dream sharing, sharing what we recall of our dreams can become a pattern at the breakfast table or at other gathering times. Expect significant guiding symbols to emerge.

Family meetings. As parents, consider establishing regular weekly family meetings at which all, including children, reflect on family life and other issues, interests, and concerns.[7] Chapter 3 of the *Rule of Benedict* addresses the subject of decision making in the monastery. Although the abbot, or parents in the case of a family, makes the final decisions on weighty matters affecting the common life, there is an admonition to invite the views of all members of the community, including the youngest. From this we learn the importance of listening respectfully to everyone affected by a common concern. Benedict noted that the Lord often reveals to the young what is best. This wisdom from the sixth-century *Rule* applies to family and our community concerns, too. Inviting all to share their views encourages fresh and creative perspectives.

> What are your usual patterns for making major decisions that affect everyone in the household? How do these patterns compare with the spiritual discernment cycle model and other resources for discernment presented here?

Church or Organization

Currently, a growing body of literature on spiritual discernment focuses on an organization's decision making. When I consulted for St. Clement's Episcopal Church in Harvey, Illinois, I recommended that spiritual discernment advisory group members read two books on the subject: *Discerning God's Will Together* by Danny Morris and Charles Olsen, and *Transforming Church Boards* by Charles Olsen. I still find these to be the most readable and helpful books on church-level spiritual discernment, with Morris and Olsen's book providing a great foundation and *Transforming Church Boards* offering practical suggestions.

My contribution to organizational spiritual discernment began with my Doctor of Ministry work with St. Clement's Church and with my subsequent thesis. Through this work I developed the spiritual discernment cycle, which provides an elegant conceptual model of discernment and emphasizes the role of emerging symbols. I also developed a successful formation program on spiritual discernment for personal and communal application, providing advanced training

To what extent is your organization or community open to the resources for spiritual discernment presented in this book?

What are the forces at work in your community that resist movement toward deeper spiritual discernment practices and what are the forces that encourage deeper use of such practices? What strategies would reduce the resistance?

of church-level discernment teams (spiritual discernment advisory groups). Teams learned practices that help elicit guiding symbols for discerning the community's focus on mission, ministry, and parish identity. These practices included dreamwork, guided imagery meditation, group *lectio divina*, journaling, and contemplative prayer while "sitting with" a question.

I have led leadership groups in several congregations and with a few organizations, parachurch and faith-based, interested in incorporating discernment principles and practices into their leadership. In this section I present more specific practices as well as examples of emerging guiding symbols that spoke to particular communal situations.

The Flying Chicken

The guidance of symbols and the collection of images in organizational life provide an important tool for communal discernment, visioning, and strategic planning. Gil Rendle, a church consultant who worked with an urban congregation that saw community involvement as an important part of its mission, urged the congregation to explore how its story fit with the biblical story. In the congregation's planning process they came to believe that God called them to "mount up with wings like eagles" (Isa. 40:31). And yet, they felt that the image of a flying chicken was more like them. They even made it into their logo:

> However, the congregation also recognized a number of times in recent history when they had the opportunity or challenge to soar as an eagle in addressing neighborhood issues but had "chickened out." Their conclusion was that they

were called to be flying chickens. Their challenge was to face their fears and mount up with wings nevertheless. As you might imagine, their perceived relation to the biblical story provided clarity and direction for their decision making over the next several years. As they faced difficult decisions, they reminded each other that it was in just such a situation that they were called to mount up and fly.[8]

Guidance from symbols finds powerful expression at St. Clement's Episcopal Church in the food imagery that kept occurring in the parish. The food pantry and clothing ministry grew to become their defining social ministry, serving the broader community of Harvey, Illinois, and the region. Nearly everyone in the church makes a contribution to this ministry, from grant writing to distribution. Eucharist at St. Clement's is the central, weekly, liturgical celebration with its powerful sacramental feeding of Christ's people with his body and blood. This feeding theme became, very appropriately, the guiding symbol for the community through the parish discernment advisory committee's work on the parish mission statement, which finally took shape as:

> St. Clement's Church strives to fulfill the command of our Lord Jesus Christ to "Feed My Sheep"—in body, mind, and spirit.
> - We feed the **body** by providing food and clothing to our community as needed, and actively inviting all to join us in our worship and fellowship.
> - We feed the **mind** by providing opportunities for all to engage in study, dialogue, and prayer around scripture, and God's purpose in our lives.
> - We feed the **spirit** by providing worship that is holy, welcoming, loving, diverse, and scriptural, and by bringing others to the knowledge and love of God, the saving power of Jesus Christ, and the comfort and blessing of the Holy Spirit.[9]

I have shared various images with leaders in seminaries, especially with my wife as she worked as academic dean at both Seabury-Western and Church Divinity School of the Pacific (CDSP). While at Seabury, I got to know all the members of the system well. The pace of work and juggling of responsibilities could get frantic. The predominant image, both visual and aural, that kept coming to my mind at Seabury was the internationally famous Flying Karamazov Brothers' juggling act. This incredible comedy team tosses strange and potentially dangerous stuff to each other in rhythm with frantic Russian music. At CDSP my wife told me that she and the seminary's president used images that included "chipping away at a brick wall" and "working on a piece of sculpture."

More on Communal Dreaming

We have seen how powerful the recurring and shifting St. Clement's church dream was in mirroring the emotional and spiritual dynamics of that congregation and in pointing to its gradual healing. In several retreats with the leadership group of other churches and a parachurch organization, I asked members if they had dreams to share. A member came forward to offer one. In these situations, I give the group some basic "rules" for engaging the dream and each other in sharing interpretations and associations. The most basic principles?

- ▸ Avoid imposing interpretations on others.
- ▸ Treat everyone's offerings respectfully.
- ▸ Allow freedom to wonder what God or Wisdom might be suggesting through the dream and the subsequent sharing of associations and interpretations.

When I offered a seminary course in group dreamwork in spring 2003—which included the Social Dreaming matrix model developed by W. Gordon Lawrence—several students presented dreams that struck us with particular force in regard to the seminary's present situation and general implications for current theological education. The dream, "Expensive Ice Cream," involved Seabury seminary students who went out to get some ice cream. When one student placed her order first but received her ice cream after many others had been served, she received a bill for $45.00. The dreamer felt outraged at the enormous bill that her fellow student was charged. Not surprisingly, along with other interpretations, students strongly resonated with this symbol of the high cost of seminary education—an important issue in the Episcopal Church as well as for higher education in general.

Another dream gave us symbols that were even more challenging to the current state of seminaries and theological education:

Seabury Geckos & Dinos

Scientists are running tests on animals at Seabury-Western Theological Seminary. There were some who seemed to have free run around the lab—these were human-sized geckos. In the center was a dome-shaped holding pen made out of glass and concrete. Dinosaurs were inside and really wanted out. One was looking around trying to figure out how to do that. The geckos surrounded the pen and watched. When I told the scientist that the dinosaurs were going to try to get out, she was unconcerned because "they were too stupid."[10]

When leaders of the seminary engaged in strategic planning in 2007, I was the chaplain of the seminary and offered that gecko dream, and questions that arose from the matrix session, to the then dean and president of the seminary, Gary Hall, writing:

This particular dream has stayed with me over the years both for its humor and the way it raises questions for me about Seabury (and the Church). Here are some questions it raises for me:

- To what extent is Seabury an institution that is capable of adaptation (free-running human-sized geckos) or will become extinct (stupid, penned-in dinosaurs)?
- How adaptive is our administration, faculty (and pedagogy), students, and trustees?
- What is at the center of Seabury?

> ▸ Are the scientists the real authorities in this age? What might they represent?

We were in the middle of a financial crisis at the seminary. Gary expressed the situation very well, remarking that we were trying to maintain a nineteenth-century model of seminary in the twenty-first century—and it no longer worked. The dream seemed to point to the challenges of that changed reality.

Seabury did evolve but not without radical structural changes. The seminary declared financial exigency and revoked faculty tenures, released its faculty and rehired only a few, eliminated its long-term residential program, divested its real property holdings, relocated, and joined in a "federated" relationship with Bexley Hall, another Episcopal seminary operating in the Midwest. Other seminaries face similar challenges.

Meditations and Imagination Exercises

I often use guided meditations or imagination exercises for churches and faith-based organizations. Though the following guided-imagery meditation may be used for personal reflection, it would be even more effective if offered in a community that included an opportunity to debrief together, for example, in a retreat that focuses on the gifts of the Spirit and ministry, or in a discussion of God's mission. The meditation draws on the call of the prophet Jeremiah.

The Word of the Lord Came to Me— Guided-Imagery Meditation

Now the word of the LORD came to me saying, "Before I formed you in the womb I knew you, and before you were born I consecrated you; I appointed you a prophet to the nations."

Then I said, "Ah, Lord God! Truly I do not know how to speak, for I am only a boy."

But the LORD said to me, "Do not say, 'I am only a boy'; for you shall go to all to whom I send you, and you shall speak whatever I command you.

> Do not be afraid of them,
>> for I am with you to deliver you,
>> says the LORD."
> Then the LORD put out his hand and touched
> my mouth; and the LORD said to me,
>> "Now I have put my words in your mouth.
>> See, today I appoint you over nations and over
> kingdoms,
>>> to pluck up and to pull down,
>>> to destroy and to overthrow,
>>> to build and to plant."
>
> Jeremiah 1:4–10

Take a moment to invite God to be with you in this meditation, guiding you and opening you to a deeper relationship with the Holy One. Be sure to pause for reflection after each movement:

1. Imagine that you are in a special place where you feel most connected to God, to your deepest, truest sense of yourself, and to the world around you. Perhaps it is a place you go for rest and renewal . . . or worship . . . or vacation. Maybe it is a place that is known only in your imagination.

2. Get as full a sense of being in that place as you are able, noticing what the place looks like and feeling yourself there. Notice also if there are other people in that place. If there are other people there and you wish to acknowledge them, feel free to do so.

3. Now imagine that Christ or the Spirit or Holy Wisdom is also in that place. The Holy One might appear to you as someone you know, male or female, or as someone you imagine from art or some other source. The Holy One might take some other form than a human being . . . perhaps a special light, a sense of warmth, an angelic form, voice or music. Imagine that the Holy One wishes to come near you and seeks your consent to approach you. Do you give consent?

4. If you consent to the Holy One drawing close to you, notice how you feel as the Holy One approaches. Listen as the Holy One tells you, "Before I formed you in the womb I knew you, and before you were born, I consecrated you." Notice how you experience those words . . . what you feel and what thoughts arise in response to the Holy One telling you, "Before I formed you in the womb I knew you, and before you were born, I consecrated you."

5. The Holy One comes to you with a concern and asks you for help. Get as clear a sense as you can for what that concern is, and what you are asked to do. Do you share that concern? Is this something you want to become involved in? Do you currently have what you need in order to respond? If not, tell the Holy One what you need and listen and look for a response.

6. Now the Holy One has something to encourage you. It may be a word or phrase, or a symbol. It may be a sound or music or a gesture. Receive whatever the Holy One has for you and feel free to ask questions and respond in any way you feel is appropriate or necessary.

7. The time has come to return to your normal consciousness, so say goodbye to the Holy One in whatever way seems fitting. Watch as the Holy One moves away from you. Observe the sense of the special place begin to fade. When you are ready, conclude your depth prayer by opening your eyes and joining us.

I developed the following meditation when asked to support the men of a church in the aftermath of a former priest's abusive activities. The interim priest, a woman, had worked with the women but thought that having a man work with the male parishioners might be helpful. This meditation was a part of the larger conversation with the men.

Healing the Soul of the Community

Be sure to pause for reflection after each movement and more frequently, if it seems appropriate:

1. Imagine you are in your church. You might be alone, but you could be with others, including spiritually mature and wise people. Even the Christ or Holy Wisdom might be present.

2. You—and any companions—wait for something that is going to appear before you, a visual representation of the soul or spirit of your church community. This "soul image" may appear to you in any form whatsoever—perhaps as a plant, an animal, a person, a spiritual being, a light, or some completely new kind of creation. Try not to force an image; accept whatever comes with interested curiosity.

3. Notice what the soul image of your church looks like:
   ▶ Observe its form . . .
   ▶ Note its coloration . . .
   ▶ How does it move?
   ▶ What is its general appearance?
   ▶ What it is doing?
   ▶ Notice also what feelings emerge by being with it.

4. If you wish, communicate with this soul image to learn more about it. Talk to any of the wise people—or with Christ—about the soul of the church.

5. Let the image show or describe the kind of wound it has from the trauma or abuse it received:
   ▶ What does the wound look like?
   ▶ Is the wound clean or dirty?
   ▶ Is there scar tissue?
   ▶ What does the soul image say or indicate has happened to the wound over time?
   ▶ What does it say it needs for further healing?

6. What do *you* think the soul image needs for healing and well-being?
   ▶ Is there anything it needs you to do?

> ▸ If you have companions, what do they say or do about the soul image's needs?
> ▸ If the Christ is present, what does the Christ say or do about further healing?

7. Ask the soul image to show you what it would look like were it fully healed.

8. When you are ready, thank the soul image for showing itself to you and your companions, and let it move away from your awareness.

9. If you have companions and/or the Christ with you, receive any final words or symbols they want to give for your community's well-being. Thank them for being with you and let them move away from your awareness.

10. When you are ready, shift your own awareness from your inner world to the outer world.

Sometimes I instruct a group—such as a church leadership group—to sit contemplatively and ask for a guiding symbol that might speak to a situation, or simply to sit with a question in prayer and await any response. Suggested instructions for that contemplative waiting follow.

Praying for and with a Guiding Symbol

Invite the group into a time of silent prayer, with or without background instrumental music, that asks God to provide guiding symbols for the group or the larger community. Symbols that emerge might include such things as:

> ▸ a passage or scene from Scripture
> ▸ a word or phrase from some other wisdom source
> ▸ a song
> ▸ an image
> ▸ a wisdom person from the spiritual tradition.

In the prayer time, group members imaginatively engage the emerging symbol in any way that seems appropriate. If a symbol does not emerge for some members, ask them to simply stay with the emptiness.

Open and close the silent, group contemplative prayer simply, perhaps using a bell, chant, or other audible signal.

Following the extended silence, invite group members to share what emerged for them as guiding symbols or qualities of emptiness, and let the group reflect upon what was received. This meditation opens us to the potential for God to provide guidance to the community.

New Testament scholar Walter Wink wrote his fascinating powers trilogy on understanding, discerning, and acting in the face of the powers and principalities in our world. Wink believes that all created things have a spirit, whether individual or corporate. Human constructs such as societies, organizations, churches, institutions, schools, corporations, and so on have spirits that reflect their being. Wink refers to the letters to the angels of the churches in the book of Revelation as examples of discerning the spirit of churches. That got me wondering about discerning the spirit or soul of an organization, church, or business. I developed a new tool for discernment, a meditation focused on interviewing the spirit of the organization. I've used this meditation in the seminary classroom in some of my small-group leadership courses, and also with several people in spiritual direction. I often provide two choices for the meditators: I can lead them in the meditation, or they can read the meditation by themselves and journal their responses. With a group, we gather to debrief on what members discovered in the "interview."

Imaginative Interview with the Spirit of the Organization

If you are doing this by yourself, read through the entire meditation before beginning. If leading a group, be sure to pause for reflection after each movement and more frequently, if appropriate.

1. Begin by praying for God to work with your imagination to give you new insight into the spirituality of your church or organization.

2. Then imagine that you are a reporter or an ethnographer interviewing the spirit of this church or organization. You enter into a dialogue with it to learn more. However, you may conclude your meditation at any time you choose, and cover only topics you feel safe exploring.

3. Be open to this spirit appearing to you in any shape or form *it* chooses. It may appear as an animal, a human, a plant, or have another familiar shape and form—but it may present itself in an unfamiliar shape and form. Observe:

- Are there other things near it?
- Does it have a particular gender?
- Notice what color or colors it exhibits. How is it adorned?
- Does it have a particular name?
- How old does it appear to be?
- What does it say its purpose is?
- Who or what does it serve?
- Who or what is it allied with?
- Who or what serves it?
- What gives it energy?
- What does it say it needs?
- How strong, healthy, and vital is it?
- What are its greatest challenges?
- What is it afraid of?
- What does it desire?
- How does it manifest its power? How does it use its power?
- How does it relate to the organization's leadership?
- How does it relate to the organization's members?
- How does it relate to the organization's constituents, if different than members?
- What does it do to those who try to change the organization?
- Does it identify with a particular biblical phrase, passage, story, or image?

> ▸ How do you relate to it—cognitively and affectively?
> ▸ What other questions do you have for it? What else would like to explore with it?

When you have completed the interview, return to your normal awareness of reality and, if you have not already done so, make notes on what you learned. Then share this with others as you think is appropriate. Although just one person can do this exercise for their own personal understanding, it can be beneficial for others to do it, too. That way there can be discussion of what similarities and differences emerge, and how that brings wisdom to the group.

In the examples of spiritual practices and dreamwork presented in this chapter and earlier (including group forms of *lectio divina*), which seem most applicable to your community? Which would be the greatest stretch for your community?

Societal and Global Concerns

BILL MOYERS: Why is a myth different from a dream?

JOSEPH CAMPBELL: Oh, because a dream is a personal experience of that deep, dark ground that is the support of our conscious lives, and a myth is the society's dream. The myth is the public dream and the dream is the private myth. If your private myth, your dream, happens to coincide with that of the society, you are in good accord with your group. If it isn't, you've got an adventure in the dark forest ahead of you.

BILL MOYERS: So if my private dreams are in accord with the public mythology, I'm more likely to live healthily in that society. But if my private dreams are out of step with the public ...

JOSEPH CAMPBELL: ... you'll be in trouble. If you're forced to live in that system, you'll be a neurotic.

BILL MOYERS: But aren't there visionaries and even leaders and heroes close to the edge of neuroticism?

JOSEPH CAMPBELL: Yes, there are.[11]

In this section we explore guiding symbols that emerge in society and the world that reveal our shared hopes, fears, aspirations, and spiritual concerns. To start, let's briefly discuss the role of myth. As implied in Bill Moyers's interview with Joseph Campbell above, there are positive and negative attributes to myths.

Social Symbols and Myths

Often in popular language when we refer to "myth" it is seen as a distortion of truth or outright lie. In religious studies, social psychology, and cultural anthropology the word *myth* is understood differently and not negatively. In those disciplines, a myth is a symbolic way that a group or culture describes what is real and valuable. In that way of understanding, myth represents a symbolic structuring of meaning and order and reveals a deep truth about the nature of reality.

For example, the book of Genesis presents two creation myths or sacred stories about the beginning of the world. Genesis 1:1–2:4a describes the creation of the whole cosmos and the earth in seven days. If we allow science to help us interpret the passage, we can say that the truth of this story of creation is not dependent on seven literal calendar days. This story tries to convey some other, deeper truth, one that encompasses the whole cosmos. Text-critical biblical scholars argue that the author or the final editor of this passage was probably from the priestly order, speaking to Jews about the importance of keeping the Sabbath. The story says that God rested from the labor of creation on the seventh day. The author *presents God as the source of all creation—the cosmos as well as the Earth—and that God originally declared all of creation, including human beings, as very good.* This has enormous implications for understanding our relationship with the Earth and the universe. This creation myth reveals that the universe was created and declared fundamentally good by a divine creator God. It is not just random happenstance that we live in this world. We are a part of something vast, wonderful, and infused with the sacred in which everything originates.

The other creation story begins with Genesis 2:4b and focuses on the Garden of Eden, especially the creation of a human being. God sets boundaries between what would and would not be allowed, creates other animal forms of life as potential helpers—who names them and therefore establishes a relationship with them—then brings forth a woman from the rib of the man as a true and equal partner. This story continues with the temptation to go beyond the boundary God had set and the fall of the couple from their initial intimate and innocent relationship with each other and with God. They lose their place in Eden. This second creation myth focuses more on the importance of right relationships—including the primary relationship with God—and the consequences of sin.

The symbols in this second story have been the focus of much theological reflection. In our time, for example, the symbol of the garden emerges as an important guide to our right relationships with the Earth. In this version of the creation event, God gives human beings the task of tilling and keeping the Earth—husbandry to help it flourish. We are responsible for the garden's well-being and development. Our purpose on this Earth, illuminated by the garden symbol, is to care for it in ecological harmony—a very different sense of our purpose on this Earth than in the first creation story, in which humans are to have dominion over everything.

The language and form of this second story indicates that the author is different from that of the first story. Both stories are mythic; that is, they both convey deep truths about the nature of the cosmos, creation, human beings, and relationship with the Divine. Both go far beyond a simple and literal reading.

What are the contemporary social and global symbols and myths of our age? What do those convey about the nature of reality in the hopes and fears that are expressed? How might we look at these symbols and myths critically and with discernment? We face many social and global symbols, and they come to us from many sources: politics, literature, television shows, movies, art, music and popular songs, religion, and other fields. We can only look at a selection drawn from such a broad spectrum.

"Boldly Go"

I'm an avid science fiction and fantasy fan, both in reading and in the visual media. When our son was growing up we had "family reading time" near the end of his day. From his childhood and up into his early teen years we read the fantasy and science fiction works of people like J. R. R. Tolkien, C. S. Lewis, Lloyd Alexander, and J. K. Rowling. We thrilled at the heroic journey portrayed in Tolkien's *Lord of the Rings* trilogy, both the books and the films by Peter Jackson, the *Star Wars* series with its mythic structure, and the deep conflict between good and evil that defined the worlds of magic and muggles in the Harry Potter series.

Which movies, television shows, or other popular media have the capacity to speak to you about important concerns and conditions in our lives?

Being a *Star Trek* "Trekkie" (fan), I appreciate the grand vision launched in the inaugural 1966 series of a spaceship crew composed of humans of different nations and races and sexes, together with intelligent beings from other worlds, working together in the common mission, in the revised language of later versions in the franchise, "to boldly go where no one has gone before." The United States was in the midst of the great civil rights movement confronting racism and locked in a bitter Cold War with the Soviet Union. The competition with Russia in space technology and exploration was underway. Feminist social and political criticism barely found traction in the dominant American culture at that time, but this grand vision of bold adventure—both for major cultural change as well as space exploration—came from the imagination of Gene Roddenberry and his staff and guided us forward into a new frontier. Was the Spirit also using these images and stories to move us to a new place? Certainly change was, and continues to be, necessary.

Racism

The reading that shaped my adolescent years and growing sense of social conscience included Ralph Ellison's 1952 novel *Invisible Man* and journalist John Howard Griffin's 1961 nonfiction book *Black Like Me*. The Rev. Dr. Martin Luther King Jr.'s speeches and nonviolent demonstrations prophetically identified the racism, embedded in personal bigotry and in the deeper social structures embedded in the dominant American economic, political, educational, religious, health, and military systems. King eloquently conveyed his dream of a just society:

> I have a dream that one day this nation will rise up and live out the true meaning of its creed: "We hold these truths to be self-evident: that all men are created equal." I have a dream that one day on the red hills of Georgia the sons of former slaves and the sons of former slave-owners will be able to sit down together at a table of brotherhood. I have a dream that one day even the state of Mississippi, a desert state, sweltering with the heat of injustice and oppression, will be transformed into an oasis of freedom and justice. I have a dream that my four children will one day live in a nation where they will not be judged by the color of their skin but by the content of their character. I have a dream today . . .[12]

Dr. King's dream of a racially just society continues to inspire us, even as we face the many ways racial bias and systematic racism persist as one of America's greatest sins, embodied in the various forms of oppression and vested privilege that run counter to the American myth as the land of "freedom and equality for all." King presented powerful symbols of transformation that provide light for the path of racial reconciliation. The "red" hills of Georgia can speak both to the color of the clay soil, a physical context in which racial tension was manifest, but also evokes the bloody social and moral losses that are a cost of racial injustice. In that physical and social setting, King envisioned a future in which the "sons" of both slaves and slave owners would sit together at a "table of brotherhood." King provided a brilliant contrast between the then-present "desert state" condition of Mississippi, suffering under the heat of racism's injustice and oppression, with a hoped-for transformation into an "oasis of freedom of justice." Here, one of the greatest orators and leaders of the civil rights movement offered compelling images and a vision for the nation that became a shared dream for whites and blacks for generations.

My internal struggle against racism became most evident to me in a dream I had in the later 1970s while working with the Department of Social Services in Michigan:

Unjust Treatment

I am walking alone in a city and come upon some white men that see me and yell, "Get him!" They start chasing me, and finally I am cornered. They come upon me and start dousing me with gasoline. I am terrified as I realize that they want to set me on fire. I break away, smelling the gasoline on me as I run. I see a squad car and run up to the car screaming for help. The men that get out of the squad car are officers of the sheriff's department, and one of them says, "You are in big trouble, son." They handcuff me and haul me away to jail. I am now in a jail cell and feel overwhelmingly depressed and hopeless.

I am told that I have a visitor. I see a black woman approach outside my jail cell; it is my wife. She, too, is grief-stricken because of how I have been treated and the hopelessness about my getting out. Suddenly I wonder about her and look at my hands and see that they are black. Ah! I realize that I am now a black man in this racist country. This is why I am being treated so unjustly.

I continue to identify with both images: the oppressor and the victim. I am, by default, an oppressor, since I live in a system that continues to favor me due to race, sex, education, and economic advantage . . . and I benefit from those advantages at the expense of the disadvantaged. I am also a victim, since I recognize this unjust condition and am (largely) an unwilling participant, although I know that the suffering caused by this system primarily falls on those who are the targets and not those who are privileged. My path toward greater liberation lies in alliance with those who suffer under oppressive systems. Ultimately, I know that true liberation for all comes only when we find release from the injustices of racism and other forms of oppression.

Apocalyptic Age

We have observed astonishing growth in the number of apocalyptic and postapocalyptic visions in movies and television since consciousness of possible global devastation by nuclear war in the 1950s and the equally devastating ecological crisis that began to be recognized in the early 1970s. Of course, apocalyptic literature and themes are not new to our era. Both Old and New Testament present visions of cataclysmic end times and wars in heaven and earth between the forces of good and evil. What fascinates me, however, is the shift, since the end of World War II and the beginning of the Cold War, toward imagining global catastrophic events *due to human responsibility*.

I grew up with the imminent threat of global nuclear war. As children in school, we practiced what to do in the event of a nuclear attack, and some of our schoolmates' parents built fallout shelters for their homes. As a fourteen-year-old during the Cuban Missile Crisis in October 1962, I recall my father preparing to be called out of military retirement if our country were brought into a dreaded World War III. As early as 1957, apocalyptic and postapocalyptic novels and movies addressing global nuclear warfare came into the public's imagination, including the movie *On the Beach* (1959), based on the 1957 novel of the same name by Nevil Shute, the novel *A Canticle for Leibowitz* by Walter M. Miller Jr., the novel *Alas, Babylon* (1959) by Pat Frank—and the Playhouse 90 movie adaptation of that book in 1960—and the 1964 films *Failsafe* and *Dr. Strangelove*. More recently, the film *Book of Eli* (2010) describes the dystopian aftermath of a nuclear apocalypse.

As the U.S. policy of nuclear deterrence moved into the insanity of mutual assured destruction (MAD), and while we citizens of the world were living with apocalyptic fear, at some time in the late 1970s

I dreamed of watching the horizon with a feeling of sad finality as a mushroom cloud produced by an exploding nuclear bomb grew over Detroit. In my dream, I recognized that it would only be a matter of time before the end came. Remembering now that warning dream, I think of the haunting ending of *On the Beach,* which shows Melbourne, Australia, deserted, abandoned, and devoid of life due to radiation poisoning or suicide. In the final shot, a church banner reads, "There Is Still Time . . . Brother."

I am a citizen of a militaristic nation. The United States' obsession with nuclear dominance and global military supremacy manifests that militarism. I fear that in a hidden but continuing myth of Manifest Destiny, or a Pax Americana drive for empire, we have projected our shadow side onto other nations and then created violent solutions for that projection. We often impose our cultural images of success, both materialistic and inflated, as the standard for all people in the world. And our definition of "national interests" likely relates to commercial enterprises, especially energy and armaments, backed up with military power. It was Dwight Eisenhower, in the final speech of his presidency in 1961, who prophetically cautioned against the rising power and danger of undue influence of the "military-industrial complex."[13]

We live in a world that accepts violence for political, ideological, and economic gain as a strategic tactic. As a nation, the devastating images of the terrorist hijacking of airplanes and the subsequent attacks on the Pentagon, the destruction of the Twin Towers and an additional building at the World Trade Center, and the crash of United Airlines Flight 93 on September 11, 2001, are burnt into our collective psyche. The images may be as powerful for this generation as were images of the attack on Pearl Harbor for our parents or grandparents. How critical it is that we bring these images of violence and hatred—along with the instinctive urges for retribution—before the guiding presence of the Divine.

Nonviolence

I struggle with being a Christian and with seeking nonviolent ways of living in my American culture that so frequently resorts to violence as the solution. My immediate family includes military officers and ordained ministers, and I respect the costs and sacrifices demanded in both forms of work. I carry within me the tension of living the way of the warrior *and* the minister of the gospel of peace. I have loved hunting with gun and bow and feeling appreciation and respect for the animal life that is given that we might live. I have also been a conscientious objector, refusing to participate in war and advocating for Christian pacifism. Am I a hypocrite? Or am I embracing the paradoxes of my humanity? Mostly I seek a path where these internal dimensions more fully integrate with and serve God's purposes in this troubled, conflicted world. I desire and participate in this work of integration, but I cannot accomplish it without the Spirit's continuing creativity within me.

In his own time and culture, Jesus clearly renounced violence as the way to overcome evil. He taught his followers to love their enemies and to do good to those that hated them. With boldness, strength, and courage, Jesus challenged what he saw as wrong. And the Gospels don't portray him as completely free of violence; all four Gospels tell the story of the cleansing of the Temple, where, morally outraged, he turned over moneychangers' tables and drove them out with a whip made of chords. This is, however, the only instance of Jesus's using physical force, even in the face of life-threatening danger. His refusal to use power and violence for his own self-defense led him to the cross. Responding to Jesus's call to follow him in the way of the cross, offering our lives and actions purposefully for God's just and liberating realm on Earth while renouncing violence, demands our fullest commitment and discernment.

I've had to deal many times with my own inner violence, characterized by anger, defensiveness, and resentment, as part of following Jesus and representing the "third way" of the peacemaker. That third way challenges me to not accommodate to coercive or unjust power and to resist using violent force against my opponent. Rather, I try to direct the anger about injustice and oppression into a creative path that leads to a peaceful outcome. One of my early dreams with postapocalyptic symbols (with apologies to Moses) provides a lively image of moving in that direction:

Breakthrough to a New World (October 1980)

I am on a train with a large number of people who have traveled to a region similar to the Badlands. We were searching for the new world, the promised land, looking for a way to break through to this new realm. We climbed hills and looked in valleys, constantly searching. The area was colorful, clay earth tones and striated hills, but essentially barren.

At one point I was told that my staff and boots were missing. I looked at my feet and saw that I was barefoot. We located the boots and walking stick, and I rejoiced at finding them. The group expressed joy too, echoing my joy. I saw that the top part of my walking stick was charred, and I noted that this must have happened at the great conflagration.

As I was searching one of the hills, the clay gave way and I was able literally to break through to a new scene, a new world. This place was far greener and meadow-like. Very pastoral. My people came with me, and we were met by several curious creatures that offered themselves as guides and allies. One creature looked rather like a huge scorpion but was very cordial in greeting us. The other was animal-like, slightly resembling a lamb, and was very friendly.

The scorpion-like creature explained to me that both creatures offered their services, and that we must choose individually which creature we preferred as our guide and companion. The "scorpion" creature would teach the skills of a fearless warrior and would serve as a strong ally and protector. The "lamb" would teach gentleness, understanding, peacefulness, and love. I told the scorpion that I have been a warrior all my life and now choose, and need to learn, the way of the lamb.

Later in life I discovered the desert elders'[14] teaching that the whole human being, reflecting the *imago Dei*—our being made in the image of God—is like a charioteer holding the reins of two powerful horses. These horses represent the natural energies within us: one horse could be thought of as "anger" and the other as "desire." The charioteer holding the reigns of these powerful horses could be thought of as "reason" in our capacity for drawing on resources that help us connect with God's purposes in the world (science, wisdom, prayer, logic, Scripture, and other sources of knowledge).

As we engage our capacity to know or discern God's purposes, we can harness and guide these energies in the service of God's kingdom. The symbols of the lamb and lion in my ministry point to the same intention of integrating these energies. We all carry within us those powerful energies, however symbolized: anger/desire horses or scorpion/lamb or lion/lamb personae. We carry those energies within us as individuals . . . and as whole societies and nations. As we recognize, own, discern, and integrate these powers, we further God's realm on Earth.

Ecological Crisis

While we have, to a limited extent, heeded the warnings of nuclear apocalypse and taken some measures to reduce its possibility, we still face our abuse of the Earth's ecosystem and its consequences, such as climate change. Warnings first surfaced through novels and movies beginning in the early 1970s. British science fiction novelist John Brunner raised an early warning with his dystopian picture of the United States in *The Sheep Look Up,* published in 1972. The year 1973 saw the release of the grim movie *Soylent Green,* offering a miserable future in which overpopulation, pollution, the greenhouse effect, and poverty combine to create a massive food crisis. The late twentieth century and beginning of the twenty-first century brought an increase in apocalyptic and postapocalyptic movies and documentaries warning of the pending ecological crisis, including *Mad Max* (1979), *Waterworld* (1995), *The Day after Tomorrow* (2004), *An Inconvenient Truth* (documentary, 2006), *Wall-E* (2008), and *Avatar* (2009).

The extensive resistance and denial around the ecological crisis and climate change both amazes and disheartens. Even the medium-term common interest dictates radical changes in governmental and industrial approaches to our environment. Yet we often seem trapped in perpetuating policies that only serve short-term interests dictated by large corporations.

Changes are difficult, and I understand that I am a privileged member of a society that consumes more goods and energy than any other country in the world. What sacrifices we in the United States should be making for the good of our planet and its people are difficult to comprehend.

And yet, our children and grandchildren are already paying the price for delays in major environmental policy reforms. Consider, for example, the increase in asthma cases among our younger generations and known links to air pollution, although risk factors include both environmental and genetic causes. The California Environmental Protection Agency reports a 75 percent increase in asthma in the United States since 1980, with children and certain racial groups, especially African Americans, experiencing relatively greater increases in asthma.[15]

Climate change indicates global warming. According to the Environmental Protection Agency:

> The global average temperature increased by more than 1.4°F over the last century. In fact, according to the National Oceanic and Atmospheric Administration (NOAA), the decade from 2000 to 2010 was the warmest on record, and 2010 was tied with 2005 as the warmest year on record. Rising global temperatures have also been accompanied by other changes in weather and climate. Many places have experienced changes in rainfall resulting in more intense rain, as well as more frequent and severe heat waves. The planet's oceans and glaciers have also experienced changes: oceans are warming and becoming more acidic, ice caps are melting, and sea levels are rising. All of these changes are evidence that our world is getting warmer.[16]

As people of faith, let's develop and enact a new covenant with the Earth.[17] This can be one of our contributions as we join with humankind to respond to our collective ecological crisis.

Dehumanization and the Limits of Science

Vampires and zombies now populate our television and movies screens and books as our social imagination reveals widespread cultural anxiety and denial about our mortality. Such "entertainment" offers metaphoric warnings about forces that feed upon our humanity, drain our energy, and threaten to make us mindless and purposeless. Human trafficking, corporate demands for cheap labor, and the entrapment of children forced to become soldiers are just a few examples of vampiric practices in our time.

Perhaps even more deeply embedded and socially accepted are the subtle ways we marginalize and objectify people, especially those with less power; we use and discard them rather than acknowledging and respecting their intrinsic value. In a country in which we preach the myth of "equal opportunity for all" and "life, liberty, and the pursuit of happiness," domestic violence, mostly perpetrated against women, persists as an epidemic.[18] Many communities make it a crime to be a homeless person forced to live in a public space.[19] The poverty rate hovers at 15 percent of the general population, with 24 percent of our children living in poverty.[20]

The symbols of vampires and zombies, like other apocalyptic themes and symbols, confront us with the limitations of science and technology to save us. These symbols reveal the hubris of claims that science owns the sole authoritative voice in understanding reality (*scientism*) and challenges the assumption that we control the consequences of our scientific and technological creations. Concern, mirrored in popular culture, for unbridled scientific applications without moral and ethical reflection go back at least to Mary Shelley's *Frankenstein*, first published anonymously in 1818.

"Tear Down This Wall!"

In West Berlin, Germany, near the Brandenburg Gate, on June 12, 1987, President Ronald Reagan gave a speech over a public-address system that could also be heard on the east side of the Berlin Wall. Reagan said, "Mr. Gorbachev, open this gate. Mr. Gorbachev, tear down this wall!" This was at a time of heightened East-West tension, as General Secretary Gorbachev sought ways to defuse tensions and relieve problems both in the Soviet Union and with the international community. It was two years later, on November 9, 1989, when the gates opened and the dismantling of the wall began. The Berlin Wall had been the prominent symbol of communism and the Iron Curtain of totalitarianism since 1961.

Other walls, both figuratively and symbolically, have been torn down and built. On the border between the United States and Mexico, walls are being built and guarded at great cost, all in the name of "protecting our border" from illegal immigrants and criminals. Is it another mask for racism? There are the walls being built separating the state of Israel from Palestinian occupied territory. Some walls divide towns and block Palestinians from ancestral farmlands and critical economic resources. Israel claims it as a defensive strategy against terrorism. Certainly, in both of these situations, the walls carry powerful symbolic weight, and we need careful discernment about what is necessary to move toward improved relationships and justice.

Other dividing walls of suspicion and intolerance have crumbled over the past several generations. One such set of walls relates to religious tolerance and understanding. Within Christianity, progress has been made in dismantling walls of denominational mistrust. The ecumenical movement, although still in process, has accomplished, with the help of the Holy Spirit, much in building relationships between denominations. There are churches, once seen as foes, now joining in various forms of ministry and mutually recognizing ministerial orders. Some share full communion with each other. Interfaith relationships have also broadened, and dialogues and agreements between the great faith traditions continue to develop when, prior to the 1960s, we had seen little mutual understanding and huge walls of separation. In a positive response to the trauma of September 11, sharing and conversations on local levels between Christians, Jews, and Muslims have increased dramatically.

On the world scene, in which racism has been systematically established in an extreme form, the dismantling of apartheid in South Africa represents a major accomplishment. The free election of Nelson

Mandela and groundbreaking nonviolent change of government is truly remarkable. The Truth and Reconciliation Commission in South Africa, as imperfect as it may have been, serves as a model for nonviolent transition of power and efforts at healing the horrendous wounds of a nation divided by race. It stands as a strong example of hope for the world, as does the U.S. effort at dismantling the wall of racism in the election of President Barack Obama. Much is yet to be done, and yet we hope that continuing efforts will bear good fruit.

Christians look to the example of Jesus Christ as the model for breaking down the wall of hostility that separates people. As Paul writes in his letter to the church in Ephesus:

> For he is our peace; in his flesh he has made both groups into one and has broken down the dividing wall, that is, the hostility between us. He has abolished the law with its commandments and ordinances, that he might create in himself one new humanity in place of the two, thus making peace, and might reconcile both groups to God in one body through the cross, thus putting to death that hostility through it. So he came and proclaimed peace to you who were far off and peace to those who were near; for through him both of us have access in one Spirit to the Father. So then you are no longer strangers and

What do you consider the most important social and global concerns of this time? What factors do you consider in determining your involvement in these matters?

What social and cultural myths and symbols do you think need critical discernment in order to determine their guiding value? What principles help you determine their value and the way they can be useful or unhelpful guides?

What spiritual practices do you now employ, or plan to use, in your personal and communal discernment around societal and global concerns?

aliens, but you are citizens with the saints and also members of the household of God, built upon the foundation of
the apostles and prophets, with Christ Jesus himself as the
cornerstone.

Ephesians 2:14–20

We face other social and global concerns than those examined
above, but these give us examples of how symbols emerge in personal
and public contexts. As Christians, we view these concerns through
the gospel of Jesus Christ. Critically and prayerfully reflecting on these
public symbols, stories, and myths from the perspective of gospel values
provides the basis for social and global discernment. We must under-
take this essential and prophetic task of discernment together. Attending to these social and global issues with discernment

- discloses our wrongdoing;
- leads us to repentance;
- guides us to proper conduct;
- lays bare our poor and disordered values;
- lets us see how we should live and what path we should take;
- warns us of the possible devastating consequences of our
  behavior;
- helps us move toward God's great desires and direction for us
  and the world.

A discerning stance helps us see how the Spirit is already at work
in our society and the world—both through the church's activities and
independent of it—and how we are to lend our support in response to
the mission of God.

5 Participating in God's Dream

Then I saw a new heaven and a new earth; for the first heaven
and the first earth had passed away, and the sea was no more.
And I saw the holy city, the new Jerusalem, coming down
out of heaven from God, prepared as a bride adorned for her
husband. And I heard a loud voice from the throne saying,
> "See, the home of God is among mortals.
> He will dwell with them as their God; they will be his peoples,
> and God himself will be with them;
> he will wipe every tear from their eyes.
> Death will be no more;
> mourning and crying and pain will be no more,
> for the first things have passed away."
And the one who was seated on the throne said, "See, I am making
all things new."

Revelation 22:1–5

DREAMS COME WITH their own inner logic, and part of that logic is that images of death and resurrection are a way of understanding and picturing the process of change. If something new is to be born, then the old must first die. In the great apocalyptic vision of John of Patmos, the first heaven and earth have passed away, and the new has come, which is the gift and work of God. It is a vision of union with the Divine, where we all belong together as God's people, God provides for us, and the old realities of suffering and death are no more. Does that mean that the world will literally have to be destroyed by fire first in order for the new to be created? No. John gives us a glimpse of God's great dream for us, in which we are now free to participate. We may enter into the new life—the new heaven and earth—*now* and trust God to work out the future.

But in order to enter into that new life, we must to the best of our ability let go of that which inhibits our true and loving relationship to God, impedes our healthy relationships with those that God made, and blocks our capacity to be in touch with our deepest self. We must seek to understand and follow God's desire. God calls us to *metanoia*, a profound repentance and conversion of our lives on an ongoing basis on all levels. Just as we can read the saying of Jesus in Luke 17:21 that "the kingdom of God is among you," or "the kingdom of God is within you," we should understand this ongoing *metanoia* of new life intimately connected to God as communal, social, global, and deeply personal. This new life is both external, consisting of a growing life of the Spirit in our expanding community relationships, and also born from internal encounters with the Spirit, that bring change.

St. Paul writes to the Christian community in Rome: "I appeal to you therefore, brothers and sisters, by the mercies of God, to present your bodies as a living sacrifice, holy and acceptable to God, which is your spiritual worship. Do not be conformed to this world, but be transformed by the renewing of your minds, so that you may discern what is the will of God—what is good and acceptable and perfect" (Rom. 12:1-2). Notice that Paul asks the people to undergo a complete change of life, one that makes them capable of discerning God's desires. Paul grounds his appeal in God's compassionate mercy, calling for an offering to God of their (and our) whole selves (body and spirit), which makes us capable of distinguishing between the worldview and lifestyle that captivates and harms us from that which is truly good, acceptable, and perfect. Paul uses the phrase "by the mercies of God"; we do not undergo this kind of radical, transformative change by ourselves alone—it is in partnership with God's power and ability to effect change in us. We bring our desire and willingness for change and for a deeper relationship with God, but we need the Spirit's power to help us along the way. On the one hand, we reject the human arrogance that claims we can and should be in complete control of our own lives and destinies, as if we were completely independent agents separated from the divine source of life. On the other hand, God invites us to accept the amazing truth that God loves us, desires us, and wants to partner with us.

Living spiritually discerning lives and actively listening for the promptings of God through emerging symbols leads to participation in the divine dream. God's wonderful, unimaginable creativity ensures the fluid and unfolding nature of that dream. When we talk of knowing God's will for us, we can avoid thinking that there is only one, fixed, static way to live our lives. God has not predetermined our destiny. Let's not put limits on God. Rather, let's dance joyfully and trustingly with our Partner into the future—into the dream.

We can understand some elements of God's dream through Holy Scripture. For example, in the Genesis creation myths, we glimpse the truth that God is at the heart of all creation, and that divine goodness blesses creation. We are challenged as human beings, all over the world, to more greatly respect all of creation and the Earth as a whole, living sacrament of God. We can resolve to be ecologically responsible. Also, in one creation story, God relates intimately with the human being (Adam) and desires for the human not to be alone but in relationship with others. This shows God's desire for us to bring respect and equality to our relationships—to God and to all humans. We ultimately connect with each other in a vast community generated by God.

In the Torah and other Hebrew writings we encounter the God who calls people to faith and into a covenantal relationship, leading them on journeys of discovery and into new lives. Some are delivered from slavery and receive the Law and gradually become shaped into a people of God, seeking a promised land. Some find hardships brought upon them by oppressors and their own sinfulness, and are led to repentance and deliverance. Their poets display a vast range of human emotions and experiences, bringing them all into the sacred Presence.

The prophets give us a vision of God's desire not only for our acknowledgment through worship but even more for the ethical demands of a God of compassion and mercy. Do we show that same compassion and mercy to those who live on the margins in our country? Do we feel outrage when our social and legal structures create oppressive and unjust systems that exploit the poor, the stranger, and the weak while favoring those who are wealthy and privileged? The prophetic vision provides hope for those who are oppressed and brokenhearted, exiled from their homeland, reminding them of a God who remains faithful to the covenant. The prophets present a picture of the divine purpose working throughout human history in the coming and going of empires. This is a God for all the nations.

The Gospels portray Jesus as one concerned for the well-being of others. His ministry demonstrates his compassion as a mirror of God's compassion. He sees his ministry as the fulfillment of Isaiah's prophecy:

> When he came to Nazareth, where he had been brought up, he went to the synagogue on the sabbath day, as was his custom. He stood up to read, and the scroll of the prophet Isaiah was given to him. He unrolled the scroll and found the place where it was written:
>
> "The Spirit of the Lord is upon me,
>> because he has anointed me
>> to bring good news to the poor.
> He has sent me to proclaim release to the captives
>> and recovery of sight to the blind,
>>> to let the oppressed go free,
> to proclaim the year of the Lord's favor."
>
> And he rolled up the scroll, gave it back to the attendant, and sat down. The eyes of all in the synagogue were fixed on him. Then he began to say to them, "Today this scripture has been fulfilled in your hearing."
>
> Luke 4:16-21,
> quoting Isaiah 61

Jesus's ministry included countless acts of healing. He healed people afflicted in their bodies, their minds, and their spirits. The miracles of the feeding of the multitudes served as a sign of a generous God who calls us to share our own abundance on behalf of those who are in need. He taught that this God forgives, loves, and freely gives mercy and grace to everyone, then calls us to do likewise. He declared that the kingdom of God has drawn near, and that God relates to us as a loving and intimate Abba-Father. And yet, as kind and compassionate as Jesus was in his life, he was not afraid to call those in religious and political places of power and authority to accountability before God's rule, challenging their hypocrisy, self-righteousness, and exploitation. Jesus's suffering and death on the cross gives us a stark image, embedded in human history, of the confrontation of evil by Jesus's discerned mission in faithfulness to his God. His resurrection from the dead provides us with the powerful symbol of God's triumph over evil and our hope of life in God beyond death.

What gives you hope in the face of major social or global issues?

What do you think is God's dream for you, for your family, your community, and your world? What does that dream look like?

In the stories in the Acts of the Apostles and other New Testament writings, we see the spread of the Holy Spirit, empowering others—Jews first and then Gentiles—for ministry and service, gathering them in the name of the Lord Jesus Christ. Concerns about discerning God's will and direction for people and churches appear in these writings.

If you were to condense your life's purpose or aspiration into a single, short sentence, what would that be?

We live in a time when we are learning to respect the deep spiritual traditions of other religious faiths, too. Jesus spoke to Nicodemus that the Spirit blows wherever it chooses.

What primary guiding symbol or image speaks to you about your life's purpose or aspiration?

We must not try to confine God to our little faith tent. Different religious traditions, including indigenous nature religions, have something important to share about our common humanity and this planet upon which we all live and depend. They ask us different questions that aid in our common discernment. They have their own spiritual practices and ways of discernment that contribute to our common fund of knowledge and wisdom. From them we receive additional guiding symbols and myths that speak to the deep truths we recognize as part of God's great dream.

So now we are taking our places in this great working-out of God's dream. As individuals, we seek what God wants for us and to know what we are to do. As couples and families, we build our lives together in deep accord with the mind of Christ, seeking to align our values and resources and choices with the kingdom of God. As communities of faith, churches, and organizations, we discern God's mission and ministry, looking deeply into our core identity, bringing our gifts and abilities with gladness to a world in need of God's love and compassion. As people of faith, we are citizens of societies and nations, wishing to know how our corporate life together conforms to God's desires for humanity. Through discernment and God's guidance, we become people firm in the knowledge of God's love, people who discover creative and compassionate paths of healing and wholeness for our world, people who challenge corrupted and oppressive powers and principalities, people who seek these powers' conversion and restoration in unity with God's purposes.

Epilogue

And [Jesus] said to them, "Therefore every scribe who has been
trained for the kingdom of heaven is like the master of a household
who brings out of his treasure what is new and what is old."

Matthew 13:52

I INVITED YOU to walk with me into the mansion that I first entered in
a dream on March 20, 2012 (p. ix). It takes courage and faith to pass the
guard dogs and cross the threshold into the mansion's dark but rich interior, where great treasures await. I believe the guardians at the threshold represent my ego; they best serve me by providing a healthy but
permeable boundary between the outer world and my inner spiritual
reality. The inner spiritual world is indeed very rich, but our Western
culture with its excessive rationalism both doubts its value and fears its
exploration, leaving depth psychologists and therapists to seek inner
healing for mental and emotional illnesses and disorders.

Inner healing has, indeed, been a positive product of the psychotherapeutic process of directed inner work. And yet inner healing need
not be the exclusive domain of psychotherapists. The church's sacramental rituals and intercessory prayer, as well as guided-imagery meditations and dreamwork, also provide conduits for the Spirit's healing
and movements toward wholeness and shalom for individuals and for
our expanding networks of relationships.

When we reserve inner work only for times when we need psychological help, we miss out on other important aspects of spiritual life,
insight, and maturity. Sadly, many mainline Christians have, for too
long, feared inner work; too anxious to look into this inner reality, they
remain immobilized. Yes, we shouldn't blithely venture into the inner
spiritual world without a sufficiently healthy ego and sense of bound-

aries around inner and outer reality. We should use available spiritual supports and guides to help us safely journey within (as well as without), with the intention of living faithfully into God's great dream and the hope that God's kingdom may come and God's will be done.

You crossed that threshold with me into that grand mansion and joined me in exploring these rich spiritual treasures, new and old. We looked at spiritual practices and ways of engaging dreams that yield powerful guiding symbols leading us to wisdom, healing, and direction. We identified tools of spiritual discernment that help us to listen for the symbolic language of God and point us to divine desire. Here we encounter God's humor, words that encourage us, pictures of our brokenness and needs for healing and reconciliation, possibilities for the future, and our yearning for love and unity. These prayer and meditation practices lead us by imagination into the inner world, and in attending to the dreams given to us from our mysterious depths, we step over the threshold and catch glimpses of God's rich and wonderful dream for us, personally and communally.

Behold the magnificent ballroom in this inner mansion. Do you hear the invitation from the Host? Join in the holy dance with the Divine in the circuitous and back-and-forth steps of spiritual discernment. As we dance, we incorporate the steps of our inner spiritual practices, reason in the service of faith, and the wisdom we receive from our spiritual friends and faith communities. While we will never be able to fully and completely grasp the wholeness and magnificence that God brings us into, let us, step by step, confidently dance by the Spirit's light into that future together.

Additional Guided Meditations and Dream Notes

Guided-Imagery Meditations

HOLY SCRIPTURE OFFERS wonderful resources for creating guided-imagery meditations. The story of the two followers of Jesus encountering him on the road to Emmaus provides a classic subject for meditation. I developed the meditation below to bring the resurrected Christ and the meditator's spiritual companions into his or her spiritual experience. Be sure to pause for reflection after each movement:

Guidance on Your Spiritual Walk

> Now on the day of the resurrection of Jesus, two of his followers were going to a village called Emmaus, about seven miles from Jerusalem, and talking with each other about all these things that had happened. While they were talking and discussing, Jesus himself came near and went with them . . .
>
> Luke 24:13–15

1. Imagine that you walk on a path. The path might be a special place for you, or it might be in an unfamiliar area.
   - Notice the qualities of the path and the surrounding area.
   - Feel the ground or pavement beneath your feet.
   - Notice the rhythm and pace of your walking.
   - Notice how you feel as you walk the path.

2. In what ways might this path reflect some spiritual dimension of your life . . . perhaps something you love . . . or desire . . . or hope for?

3. Now imagine that you invite another person (or other people) to join you on this path—someone with whom you can share deeply about life and life's direction.

- Who is this person that you would have join you?
- What qualities in him or her do you admire and appreciate?

4. Imagine this person joins you on your walk. Be with your walking companion in any way you wish.

- Are things happening in your life that you'd like to share with the other person?
- You may share whatever is on your heart and mind.
- They will listen attentively to you.

5. Imagine that in the telling of your heart's desire and in the deep listening of your companion, Christ or Holy Wisdom becomes present, too. Perhaps your companion is the outward expression of Divine Wisdom already present, or maybe Christ or Sophia appears as another person in your traveling party.

- What happens to you as you become aware of the Divine Presence walking with you?

6. What questions might Christ or your spiritual companion ask of you? What new ideas do they bring up for you to consider? What words, phrases, images, or feelings come to you as guidance?

7. The time approaches when this part of the inner journey draws to a close. Say goodbye to your traveling companion and Christ or Holy Wisdom in any way that seems right to you. Remember that you can invite them to join you again another time on your inner journey.

8. When you feel ready, return to the outer world and this gathering of God's people.

In one of the meditations I love to offer on retreat or in small groups, we travel to "the house of the Wise One." Wisdom holds an important place in the Hebrew Scriptures, sometimes personified as the female consort to God, present at the beginning of creation. The early church fathers saw this figure as Christ. This meditation gives us the opportunity to journey where Wisdom resides deep within us. Be sure to pause for reflection after each movement:

Meeting the Inner Wise One

> Wisdom has built her house,
>   she has hewn her seven pillars,
> She has slaughtered her animals, she has mixed her
>   wine,
>   she has also set her table.
> She has sent out her servant girls, she calls
>   from the highest places in town,
> "You that are simple, turn in here!"
>   To those without sense she says,
> "Come, eat of my bread
>   and drink of the wine I have mixed.
> Lay aside immaturity, and live
>   and walk in the way of insight."
>
> Proverbs 9:1–6

1. Close your eyes, if you are comfortable doing so. Imagine you are in a green meadow.
2. Look around.
   - Notice what you see and feel.
   - Notice how the ground feels below your feet.
3. Notice that a narrow dirt path leads up a small hill. Walk on that path, up the hill, to the place where the Wise One lives.
4. When you reach the door to the house of the Wise One, knock at the door and enter when you are bidden to do so.
5. Look around the room.

- ▸ What do you see?
- ▸ Look at the Wise One. Who or what does the Wise One look like?

6. You may have a question for the Wise One . . . or you might wish to tell the Wise One about something that you are now considering.

- ▸ Ask the Wise One's counsel on whatever you wish, and listen for the reply.
- ▸ If you need further clarification, feel free to engage in further conversation with the Wise One.

7. The Wise One explains that she or he has something for you. It might be a special word or phrase for you to take with you, an object, a song, or some other gift.

- ▸ Receive the gift the Wise One has for you; feel free to ask about it if you need to know more.
- ▸ Respond to the Wise One's gift in whatever way you think is appropriate.

8. It is now time to say farewell to the Wise One. Do so, and then go to the door. Walk down the hill path . . . to the meadow . . . remembering your time with the Wise One and the gift you received, knowing also that you can visit your inner Wise One again.

9. Whenever you are ready, open your eyes and bring your attention back to your outer world and this place.

My dream about the mansion and its guard dogs (p. ix) encouraged the writing of this book. In the epilogue, I observed that you joined me in the mansion (p. 165). Together we explored its riches. Come with me one final time as we venture further into that mansion. Be sure to pause for reflection after each movement:

The Dream Mansion

1. Imagine that you are walking up to a mansion, which someone invited you to visit.

> ▸ Do you arrive alone or does someone accompany you?
>
> ▸ What does the mansion look like from the outside as you approach it?
>
> 2. Who meets you at the entrance? How are you greeted?
>
> 3. Your Host grants permission to look around. If you wish, your Host will accompany you. Do you want the Host to be your guide, or do you prefer to look around alone?
>
> 4. What do you see or hear that attracts your attention?
>
> ▸ If you have a companion and/or the Host with you, feel free to discuss anything in mansion with them.
>
> 5. There are various treasures and riches in the mansion. These represent a rich spiritual life and ways of being in connection with the mansion's Host. Which of these treasures and riches do you already possess?
>
> 6. Are there additional treasures that the Host wants to share with you?
>
> ▸ If you wish to receive from the Host symbols of those treasures, do so.
>
> ▸ Again, feel free to discuss anything with the Host or your companion.
>
> 7. When you are ready to leave the mansion, thank the Host in any way that seems appropriate to you. Be sure to take any symbols from your "dream" mansion that you wish to bring into your normal awareness and life.

Dream Notes

When first reading about working with dreams, I was astonished at how many creative expressions had come from those who had paid attention to their dreams. Here are just a few examples from fields other than religion and spirituality:

Science. Friedrich Kekulé had two dreams that led to major discoveries. One dream helped him create his structure theory of the tetrava-

lent nature of carbon. He discovered the molecular structure of ben-
zene from a dream of a snake swallowing its tail.

Albert Einstein, as an adolescent, dreamed about sledding. His
dream, which occurred sometime between 1890 and 1895, became the
basis for his theory of relativity:

> I was sledding with my friends at night. I started to slide
> down the hill but my sled started going faster and faster. I
> was going so fast that I realized I was approaching the speed
> of light. I looked up at that point and I saw the stars. They
> were being refracted into colors I had never seen before. I
> was filled with a sense of awe. I understood in some way that
> I was looking at the most important meaning in my life.

Looking back near the end of his life, Einstein said, "I knew I had to understand that dream and you could say, and I would say, that my entire
scientific career has been a meditation on my dream."[1]

Applied technology. A wonderful story relates to the invention of the
sewing machine. In 1845, Elias Howe had a nightmare of being captured by natives and put in a big pot. The natives danced around the pot
and repeatedly thrust their spears at him. He noticed in this terrifying
dream that each spear had a hole at the tip. Upon waking, he then knew
where the hole for the sewing machine needle had to be placed and was
able to finalize his design.

Music. Many classical composers, included Mozart and Beetho-
ven, credited dreams as a source for their music. For example, at age
twenty-one, Italian violinist and composer Giuseppe Tartini (1692–
1770) dreamed he had sold his soul to the devil, who received Tartini's
violin and played for him:

> I heard him play with consummate skill a sonata of such ex-
> quisite beauty as surpassed the boldest flights of my imagi-
> nation. I felt enraptured, transported, enchanted; my breath

was taken away, and I awoke. Seizing my violin I tried to retain the sounds I heard. But it was in vain. The piece I then
composed, The Devil's Sonata, was the best I ever wrote, but
how far below the one I heard in my dream![2]

In contemporary music, dreams also are a fertile source for popular songs. The website for *Rolling Stone* notes that Keith Richards woke
from a dream with the riff for the famous song "(I Can't Get No) Satisfaction."[3] The online service *Songfacts* has compiled a huge list of songs
derived from the dream material of popular artists including Jimi Hen-
drix, The Beatles, Don McClean, Billy Joel, Megadeth, Fleetwood Mac,
David Bowie, Roy Orbison, Kenny Loggins, Barenaked Ladies, B. B.
King, and Faith Hill.[4]

Literature. Mary Shelley received the inspiration for *Frankenstein*
from one of her dreams while participating in a creative-writing competition. Robert Louis Stevenson, as many are aware, used his dreams as
the source of much of his writing. He had been plagued by nightmares
as a child and as a young adult, but he learned to draw on their creative value to transform them into writing. He would dream of brown-
ies performing plays on stage. He then used that material, crafting it
into such masterworks as *The Strange Case of Dr. Jekyll and Mr. Hyde.*
Contemporary horror writers Stephen King and Anne Rice credit their
dreams for inspiring their stories.

The point? Most adults in our culture undervalue their dreams; we
have the opportunity to change that perception. I have observed the
many ways in which dreams and other ways of cultivating and engaging powerful symbols can play an important role in decision making
and spirituality. We needn't see this as rational versus irrational decision-making. Rather, we use our careful thought to creatively harvest
the wisdom from other ways of knowing, such as dreams and meditations. We bring head and heart together to increase our receptivity to
divine, guiding wisdom.

In chapter 2 (p. 42), I presented questions for assessing a potential
guiding symbol. In addition to those questions, I find the work of Kelly

Bulkeley, a scholar and dream researcher, helpful. He has written extensively on dreamwork, spirituality, and religious meaning. Bulkeley offers the following general "guiding hermeneutic (interpretive) principles" for working with dreams:

- ▸ We encounter a dream as a special kind of text, as something both strange and yet related to us.
- ▸ We have a preliminary awareness of our subjective biases.
- ▸ We are open to the dream and admit to not knowing what exactly will come of the interpretation.
- ▸ We play with the dream, surrendering to a back-and-forth dialogue with it.
- ▸ The criteria for a valid interpretation are how well the interpretation harmonizes the parts of the dream with the whole, how well it coheres with the rest of our knowledge, and how well it "works out" according to our practical needs and interests.
- ▸ The ultimate goal of dream interpretation is to broaden horizons, open up new questions, and widen awareness.

He then continues with the following questions related to religious meaning and dream interpretations:

- ▸ What are the most prominent images in the dream?
- ▸ Do the images metaphorically express religious or existential concerns?
- ▸ What is the emotion power of the dream?
- ▸ Does the dream relate to a current life crisis or transition?
- ▸ Does the dream relate to both the dreamer's past and the dreamer's future?
- ▸ What potential does the dream have to transform the dreamer's waking life?[5]

Allow me again to emphasize that exploring dreams typically uncovers levels of possible meaning. No interpretation is wrong for the one who sees that meaning; likewise, more than one interpretation may be right. These levels of meaning can range from the personal to the global and the spiritual. Here are some of the multiple levels of meaning in dreams, ranging from the personal to the collective:

- *Physical health level*—symbols for and/or commentary on health
- *Humor level*—look for dream puns and "Freudian slips"
- *Personal relationships level*—explores emotional energy in past and present relationships, sexual/libidinal desire (Freud)
- *"Will to power and competence" level*—explores hopes, plans, projects, goals, dominance or submission in work and other areas of interest (Adler)
- *Personal integrative level*—various images and persons in dream are parts of the whole self (Gestalt)
- *Extrasensory perception level*—experiences of telepathy, clairvoyance, and precognition
- *Creative level*—source of solutions to personal or collective problems and source of artistry and breakthroughs in science and technology
- *Societal level*—dream includes symbols of shared social experience and global concerns, incorporating community concerns and challenges (including "Social Dreaming matrix," W. Gordon Lawrence)
- *Archetypal symbols level*—explores deep instinctual dimension of shared human drama within the "collective unconscious" (Jung)
- *Spiritual development level*—numinous encounters with the holy (and evil) in personal or collective dimensions; source of inspiration, repentance, revelation, discernment, and prophecy

Participate as a member of a dream-valuing culture. Share your dreams with others and invite them to share theirs with you. Let that be part of your morning breakfast-table talk; or, when you see someone who appeared in one of your dreams, let him or her know.

In my spiritual direction practice, many people have found meaning and direction from our work together exploring dream symbols. That has been the case for me, too, when I bring a dream or a meditation symbol to my own spiritual director and we, together, explore its wisdom. Groups for dreamwork extend that culture beyond one-to-one sharing. I can unreservedly state that participating in a dreamwork group, where members feel safe to reflect on the meaning of their own dreams and those of other members, leads to amazing and creative adventures in building a spiritual-wisdom community. Such a community simultaneously supports and transcends religious affiliations—divine wisdom can't be confined to a particular tribe.

If you are a leader in your faith community, lead the governing board in guided-imagery meditations, group forms of *lectio divina,* and other practices to encourage the emergence of guiding symbols. Don't be afraid to ask your members about dreams that may speak to the community. Such prophetic practices still provide light for the path we walk in partnership with God's purposes.

Harvest the creative fruit of dreams for your waking life. One contemporary writer on spirituality and dreamwork, Jeremy Taylor, argues that *all* dreams serve our health and wholeness.[6] Sometimes the dream can be difficult, even frightening, and we might well question whether it serves any purpose. Dreams may call us to own things about ourselves that we want to cover up or ask us to recognize powerful feelings stirring below the surface. Reflection on the symbols and their meaning can bring new understanding and awareness, guiding us to new levels of healing and integration.

As you practice bringing the gifts from your dreams into your waking life, your dreams become more vivid as you increase your ability to remember them. Keeping a dream journal increases your dream recall and the dreams' vividness. Consider praying for dreams that help illuminate a particular discernment situation. You might also hold the conscious intention to dream about a situation as you prepare to fall asleep.

If, when dreaming, you become aware that you are dreaming, create an intention about what you wish to do in your dream. This is a particular value of lucid dreaming—you *can* exercise some conscious control over the direction of your dream . . . or even change the setting of the dream to better suit your intention. For example, if you were to become lucid, that is, consciously aware you are dreaming, ask someone in your dream for help in a discernment situation or, in the dream, visit someone that represents holy wisdom to you. Ask that person for guidance. Treat lucid dreaming similarly to a self-guided imagery meditation.

In your waking state, reenter a dream as a guided-imagery meditation, continuing to work with it and further developing it. Imaginatively "talk" to the important symbols in your dream, getting more information from the symbol about its meaning and the wisdom it has for you. The symbol doesn't have to be a person—it can be something seemingly inanimate like a rock, a building, or a cave. It can still impart information about why it is there. Talk to it respectfully using the active imagination practice discussed in chapter 3 (p. 62).

We can also critically engage the cultural dreams (the myths) and challenges of our time, prayerfully seeking God's guidance. We can put those cultural mythic symbols to the test against the inherited and continually discerned wisdom gleaned from the gospel of Jesus Christ and the spiritual practices drawn from our faith traditions. The emerging guidance we can receive brings us deeper into our part as individuals and as communities in God's big dream for humanity and the world.

Bibliography

Bohler, Carolyn Stahl. *Opening to God: Guided Imagery Meditation on Scripture.* Pathways in Spiritual Growth. Rev. ed. Nashville: Upper Room, 1996.

Brockman, Pat. *The Community Dream: Awakening the Christian Tribal Consciousness.* Boulder, CO: Woven Word Press, 2000.

Bulkeley, Kelly. *Transforming Dreams: Learning Spiritual Lessons from the Dreams You Never Forget.* New York: John Wiley & Sons, 2000.

———. *The Wilderness of Dreams: Exploring the Religious Meanings of Dreams in Modern Western Culture.* Albany: State University of New York Press, 1994.

Campbell, Joseph. *Myths to Live By.* New York: Bantam Books, 1988.

Campbell, Peter A., and Edwin M. McMahon. *Bio-Spirituality: Focusing as a Way to Grow.* 2d ed. Chicago: Loyola Press, 1997.

Cepero, Helen. *Journaling as a Spiritual Practice: Encountering God through Attentive Writing.* Downers Grove, IL: InterVarsity Press, 2008.

Coughlin, Patricia. "Dreamsharing and Communal Conversion." D.Min. thesis, Christian Theological Seminary, Chicago, June 2002.

de Mello, Anthony. *Sadhana, a Way to God: Christian Exercises in Eastern Form.* Garden City, NY: Image Books, 1984.

Dorff, Francis. *Simply Soul Stirring: Writing as a Meditative Practice.* Mahwah, NJ: Paulist Press, 1998.

Fleming, David L. *The Spiritual Exercises of St. Ignatius: A Literal Translation and a Contemporary Reading.* St. Louis: Institute of Jesuit Sources, 1978.

Forest, Jim. *Praying with Icons.* Maryknoll, NY: Orbis Books, 2006.

Garfield, Patricia. *Creative Dreaming.* 2d ed. New York: Touchstone, 1995.

Hahn, Celia Allison. *Uncovering Your Church's Hidden Spirit.* New York: Alban Institute, 2001.

Halpin, Marlene. *Imagine That! Using Phantasy in Spiritual Direction.* Dubuque, IA: William C. Brown, 1982.

Johnson, Luke Timothy. *Scripture and Discernment: Decision Making in the Church.* Nashville: Abingdon Press, 1996.

Judy, Dwight H. *Discerning Life Transitions: Listening Together in Spiritual Direction.* A Spiritual Directors International Book. Harrisburg, PA: Morehouse Publishing, 2010.

Julian of Norwich. *Showings.* Translated from the critical text with an introduction by Edmund Colledge and James Walsh. The Classics of Western Spirituality. New York: Paulist Press, 1978.

Jung, Carl G. *Memories, Dreams, Reflections*. New York: Vintage Books, 1965.

Kelsey, Morton. *Discernment: A Study in Ecstasy and Evil*. New York: Paulist Press, 1978.

———. *God, Dreams, and Revelation: A Christian Interpretation of Dreams*. Revised and expanded ed. Minneapolis: Augsburg, 1991.

———. *The Other Side of Silence: Meditation for the Twenty-first Century*. Revised and updated ed. New York: Paulist Press, 1997.

———. *Transcend: A Guide to the Spiritual Quest*. New York: Crossroad, 1981.

Larsen, Stephen. *The Shaman's Doorway: Opening the Mythic Imagination to Contemporary Consciousness*. New York: Harper Colophon, 1977.

Lawrence, W. Gordon. *Introduction to Social Dreaming: Transforming Thinking*. New York: Karnac, 2005.

———. *Social Dreaming at Work*. New York: Karnac, 1998.

———, ed. *Experiences in Social Dreaming*. New York: Karnac, 2003.

Liebert, Elizabeth. *The Way of Discernment: Spiritual Practices for Decision Making*. Louisville: Westminster John Knox Press, 2008.

MacBeth, Sybil. *Praying in Color: Drawing a New Path to God*. Brewster, MA: Paraclete Press, 2007.

McIntosh, Mark A. *Discernment and Truth: The Spirituality and Theology of Knowledge*. New York: Crossroad, 2004.

Morris, Danny E., and Charles M. Olsen. *Discerning God's Will Together: A Spiritual Practice for the Church*. Nashville: Upper Room Books, 1997.

Olsen, Charles M. *Transforming Church Boards into Communities of Spiritual Leaders*. New York: Alban Institute, 1995.

Paintner, Christine Valters. *Eyes of the Heart: Photography as a Christian Contemplative Practice*. Notre Dame, IN: Sorin Books, 2013.

Paintner, Christine Valters, and Betsey Beckman. *Awakening the Creative Spirit: Bringing the Arts to Spiritual Direction*. A Spiritual Directors International Book. Harrisburg, PA: Morehouse Publishing, 2010.

Prechtel, Daniel L. "To Have the Mind of Christ: Symbol Guidance and the Development of Communal Spiritual Discernment Processes for Parish Life, Mission, and Ministry." D.Min. thesis, Seabury-Western Theological Seminary, Evanston, Illinois, May 2002.

———. *Where Two or Three Are Gathered: Spiritual Direction for Small Groups*. Harrisburg, PA: Morehouse Publishing, 2012.

Ronnberg, Ami, editor-in-chief, and Kathleen Martin, ed. *The Book of Symbols: Reflections on Archetypal Images*. The Archive for Research in Archetypal Symbolism. Cologne, Germany: Taschen, 2010.

Sanford, John A. *Dreams: God's Forgotten Language*. New York: Crossroad, 1982.

———. *The Kingdom Within: The Inner Meaning of Jesus' Sayings*. Rev. ed. Nashville: HarperCollins, 1987.

Taylor, Jeremy. *Where People Fly and Water Runs Uphill*. New York: Time Warner, 1992.

Teresa of Ávila. *The Interior Castle*. Translated by Kieran Kavanaugh and Otilio Rodrigues. The Classics of Western Spirituality. Mahwah, NJ: Paulist Press, 1979.

Wink, Walter. *The Powers That Be: Theology for a New Millennium*. New York: Galilee Doubleday, 1998.

———. *Transforming Bible Study*. Nashville: Abingdon Press, 1988.

Wuellner, Flora Slosson. *Prayer, Stress, and Our Inner Wounds*. Nashville: Upper Room, 1985.

Notes

Introduction

1. Unless otherwise noted all Scripture quotations are from the New Revised Standard Version of the Bible.

2. Quoted in the preface of *The Book of Symbols: Reflection on Archetypal Images* (Cologne, Germany: Taschen, 2010), 6.

3. "Liminal" describes a transitional situation in which we are entering something new and not yet complete. The "limin" is a threshold at a door that is crossed through to get to a new place.

4. I am particularly drawn to Tilden Edward's discussion of the word contemplative as "attention to our direct, loving, receptive, trusting presence for God. This attention includes the desire to be present through and beyond images, thoughts, and feelings" (Tilden Edwards, *Living in the Presence: Spiritual Exercises to Open Our Lives to the Awareness of God* [New York: HarperCollins, 1994], 2).

Chapter 1: Symbols and Their Kin

1. From the selected writings by James Hillman, *A Blue Fire*, introduced and edited by Thomas Moore (New York: HarperPerennial, 1991), 25.

2. I want to acknowledge with gratitude a series of teachings on atonement theories by the Rev. David Musgrave presented at St. Augustine's Episcopal Church, Wilmette, Illinois, in March 2006.

3. This active understanding of *remembrance* (*anamnesis*) is also present in Jewish Passover celebrations.

4. See also Jeremiah's anticipation of a new covenant directly written on human hearts in Jeremiah 31:31–34.

5. I refer you to Morton Kelsey's work for such an exhaustive treatment. He is introduced in the final section of this chapter.

6. Julian of Norwich, *Showings*, The Classics of Western Spirituality (New York: Paulist Press, 1978), chap. 51 (long text).

7. Besides the classic thirty-day retreat there are now opportunities for eight-day retreats, and yearlong (19th Annotated) processes of engaging the *Spiritual Exercises*.

8. Sr. Pat Coughlin, O.S.B., Institute of Spiritual Companionship (Wilmette, Illinois) presentations on March 25 and April 8, 1999, on Ignatian spirituality.

9. David L. Fleming, S.J., *The Spiritual Exercises: A Literal Translation and a Contemporary Reading* (St. Louis: Institute of Jesuit Sources, 1978), second contemplation.

10. Ibid., 110–13. These are the three rules of the second way of making a correct and good choice.

11. Margaret Silf gives other suggestions when in times of debilitating desolation. For example, remember a project that "really fired your imagination" and draw upon the positive energy even if you don't want to act upon it yet. Or, "Stay with the decisions you made, the dreams you dreamed when in consolation, even though you really feel like giving up on life" (Margaret Silf, *Inner Compass: An Invitation to Ignatian Spirituality* [Chicago: Loyola Press, 1999], 67).

12. In Christian tradition I suggest Mechthild of Magdeburg, Hildegard of Bingen, Teresa of Ávila, John of the Cross, Meister Eckhart, and the anonymous author of *The Cloud of Unknowing*, Francis of Assisi, and the Sayings of the Desert Fathers (and Mothers). In other faith traditions, for which I claim much more limited familiarity, I recommend Rabindranath Tagore, Rabia of Basra, Jalaludin Rumi, Shams-ud-din Muhammad Hafiz, Kabir, the powerful Bhagavad Gita, Lao Tzu, Chuang Tzu, and the teachings of the Hasidic master rebbes. My daughter would remind me of the yoga sutras of Patanjali with commentary by Sri Swami Satchidananda.

13. It could be argued that a "modern" suspicion of the worth of dreams as a source of revelation goes back much further to the rise of the academy in the twelfth century.

14. A full discussion about the fields of psychology and neurobiology and their interface with spirituality and discernment is beyond the scope of this book, but the following comments are pertinent to this study.

The late James Hillman and his *archetypal psychology* is viewed as either an extension of Jung's ideas about the archetypes and psychological theory or as a radical departure from it. Whether extension or departure, his psychological theory is radical and controversial. He argues for the primacy of imagination, myth, and art in depth psychology. He draws on Greek mythology in his discussion of archetypal powers, imagining a polytheistic realm of the psyche (soul), and thus argues for a "polytheistic psychology" (which he differentiates from theological polytheism). His inquiry, like Jung before him, looks at collective dimensions of the influence of archetypes in culture, positing the *anima mundi*—the soul of nature, culture, and the world.

Gestalt psychology provides a helpful approach to symbols and dreamwork. From a gestalt perspective all of the symbols in a dream are part of the person and yet have their own life. A rock, for instance, that shows up as an image in a dream can be interviewed by active imagination or role-play so the dreamer can learn more about what the rock has to say about that part of himself or herself.

Behavioral psychology has made important therapeutic interventions to help people change unhealthy behaviors. However, the theory tends to a mechanistic and reductionist understanding of people that excludes a positive role for spirituality and the divine.

Developmental psychology, which theorizes stages and developmental tasks in personal growth, provides useful theoretical models applied to spiritual and faith development.

Object-relations theory enriches our appreciation for how our images, including the way we imagine God, develop and change.

Transpersonal psychology, and the *integral psychology* of Ken Wilbur, provide a range of theories about aspects of experience that extend beyond the personal or individual to humanity and the cosmos. These writers work to integrate psychology with spiritual and mystic experience.

Neuroscience has made fascinating inroads to understanding how our human nervous system and brain function. Often this insight is linked to other fields of science and study with important results. Neuroscience, for example, would study the biological basis for how symbols emerge and affect us. One of the dangers is, like in behavioral psychology, to consider the "mind" and "consciousness" as completely a product of the nervous system and the brain—as wonderful and complex as that may be—and to limit neuroscience to a mechanistic model. Within neuroscience the most controversial proponent of the mind and consciousness not being limited to brain function is neurosurgeon Eben Alexander. In *Proof of Heaven*, Alexander describes his near-death experience and contends that, when he should not have had consciousness because of a coma, he had vivid experiences of a heavenly reality. His later writing brings in accounts of others' near death experiences as well as supporting testimony from scientific and religious sources.

15. *God, Dreams, and Revelation: A Christian Interpretation of Dreams* was again revised and expanded in 1991.

16. First published in 1976 and completely revised and updated in 1997 as *The Other Side of Silence: Meditation for the Twenty-First Century*.

17. O. Carl Simonton, Stephanie Matthews Simonton, and James Creighton, *Getting Well Again: The Bestselling Classic about the Simontons' Lifesaving Self-Awareness Techniques* (New York: Bantam, 1992), 237ff.

18. Also see my book *Where Two or Three Are Gathered: Spiritual Direction for Small Groups* (Harrisburg, PA: Morehouse Publishing, 2012), for local, church-based training of small group leaders for facilitating spiritual companionship groups of various kinds.

Chapter 2: Spiritual Guidance and Discernment

1. Prechtel, *Where Two or Three Are Gathered*, 173–74. Besides the advanced discernment training session mentioned, I have used this meditation at a seminary

community event and for a Lutheran church's board retreat. Important material for reflection and discernment emerged in each of these situations.

2. Daniel L. Prechtel, "To Have the Mind of Christ: Symbol Guidance and the Development of Communal Spiritual Discernment Processes for Parish Life, Mission, and Ministry," D.Min. thesis (Seabury-Western Theological Seminary, Evanston, Illinois, May 2002), 1–3.

3. From lectures by Wendy Wright on Salesian spirituality at the Upper Room's Academy for Spiritual Formation, November 1989. Also see the introduction by Wendy Wright in Francis de Sales, *Jane de Chantal: Letters of Spiritual Direction*, Classics of Western Spirituality (Mahwah, NJ: Paulist Press, 1988), 40–43.

4. Prechtel, "To Have the Mind of Christ," 10.

5. Thomas H. Green, S.J., *Weeds among the Wheat Discernment: Where Prayer and Action Meet* (Notre Dame, IN: Ave Maria Press, 1983), 174.

6. Churches may use different terms for their governing boards. Other organizations have governing boards that look at similar questions.

7. For example, see Galatians 5:19–23, in which the "works of the flesh" are contrasted with the "fruit of the Spirit."

8. The affirmative way (kataphatic) and negative way (apophatic) are poles of experience both of God and of our capacity to understand and relate to God in prayer. I give many examples of prayer and meditation practices that exhibit characteristics of the "affirmative way," in which things are revealed about God and our spiritual path. But there is also the hiddenness or mystery or ineffability of God that is also part of Christian spiritual experience of the "negative way." Here practices such as silence, fasting, centering prayer, and prayers of the heart—practices that emphasize letting go of our pretension to knowledge and entering into the mystery of God, simply being present in humility—are valued as spiritual resources. I explore the negative way (apophatic) dimension of spiritual life and its implications for discernment later in the chapter.

9. "The Spiritual Discernment Cycle" is based on my D.Min. thesis, and here I have reworked it without changing the substance, adding some material and changing placement of the discussion of the central section of the graph.

10. In considering the possible source, we can again look at what seems to be the fruit that the "spirit" produces. Galatians 5:19–23 contrasts "the works of the flesh" (fornication, impurity, licentiousness, idolatry, sorcery, enmities, strife, jealousy, anger, quarrels, dissensions, factions, envy, drunkenness, carousing, and things like these) with the "fruit of the Spirit" (love, joy, peace, patience, kindness, generosity, faithfulness, gentleness, and self-control). In the tradition of the desert elders in the early centuries of Christian hermits and monastics, a spiritual psychology developed that was interested in discerning the source of thoughts. Evagrius of Pontus and his disciple John Cassian believed that some thoughts arise naturally out of our human state, but others originate from demonic or divine inspiration. Out of this way of looking at sources of thought came the listing

of eight evil thoughts (precursors to the seven deadly sins) of gluttony, impurity (lust), avarice (greed), sadness (a spiritual depression), anger, acedia (boredom that leads to despair and indifference), vainglory (or envy), and pride. Against these demonic influences are the divine inspirations prompting us to eight virtues: temperance, chastity, generosity, wisdom, mildness, diligence, happiness, and humility.

11. "Paschal mystery" comes from the Greek *pascha* derived from the Aramaic and Hebrew word for "passing over." In Jewish experience of the exodus, the angel of the Lord passed over the households of the Jews but killed the firstborn of the Egyptians. The Passover feast remembers God's deliverance of the Jews. In Christian usage, the holy Eucharist celebrates the paschal mystery in which Jesus Christ is our Passover.

12. Book of Common Prayer, 302–3.

13. Besides the references to books by Scott Peck and Morton Kelsey, I recommend Avery Brooke's treatment of deliverance ministry in *Healing in the Landscape of Prayer* and the second edition of a Church of England book by the Christian Deliverance Study Group, *Deliverance: Psychic Disturbances and Occult Involvement*, edited by Michael Perry (1996). These books primarily focus on individual needs, but the problem of evil is also embedded in social structures and in global issues. Walter Wink, in books on the powers, is a good place to start on discernment and resisting evil with a larger perspective in mind. Charles Campbell's *The Word before the Powers: An Ethic of Preaching* draws on Walter Wink and William Stringfellow in dealing with these broader dimensions of evil.

14. Elsie Landstrom, "Song to My Other Self," quoted in Elizabeth O'Connor, *Our Many Selves: A Handbook for Self-Discovery* (New York: Harper & Row, 1971).

15. Why an old woman? Perhaps it was unconscious and repressed misogyny, or the dark mythic image, continuing as a social stereotype, of the witch, crone, or hag that has subversive black magical and emotional power and victimizes others. Or it could be my suspicion at that time of the wise anima archetype within me that became my shadow. All of these possibilities in turn reflect an underlying context of the social/political/spiritual destructiveness of a patriarchal system in which we live and its oppression of women. There is also likely ageism in the symbol, too. I also had a grandmother that I considered "evil" in a clinical sense, as described in Scott Peck's *People of the Lie: The Hope for Healing Human Evil*, when some people are deeply manipulative. All the above interpretations hold some truth for me.

16. Especially "Exercise 13: Finding God in All Things," in Anthony de Mello, S.J., *Sadhana, a Way to God: Christian Exercises in Eastern Form* (Garden City, NY: Image Books, 1984).

17. Prechtel, "To Have the Mind of Christ," 40–41, 82.

18. Quoted from Bonaventure's *Life of Francis* in the blog by Rocco Palmo, whispersintheloggia.blogspot.com/2010/10/rebuild-my-church.html.

19. Thomas Merton, *Thoughts in Solitude* (Kent, England: Burns & Oates, 1975), 81.

20. Told at a Christian Education Conference at Kanuga Conference Center in the late 1970s by Megan McKenna.

21. Psalms 27, 30, 88, and 31 are from the Psalter in The Book of Common Prayer (1979).

22. Parker J. Palmer, *Let Your Life Speak: Listening for the Voice of Vocation* (San Francisco: Jossey-Bass, 2000), 38.

23. Carolyn Stahl Bohler, "Finding a Buried Treasure," in *Opening to God: Guided Imagery Meditation on Scripture* (Nashville: Upper Room Books, 1996), 58–59.

Chapter 3: Practices for Inviting the Emergence of Guiding Symbols

1. Closely connected to this practice of holy silence, one of my spiritual companions reminds me, is the fourth of the Ten Commandments—keeping the Sabbath day holy. Setting aside a day a week for rest and relationship to God is a spiritual practice that clears away distractions and avoidance.

2. Before that, in the Gospels we read of Jesus going to places of solitude for prayer, and to the desert for fasting and vigil. Or consider the stories in Hebrew Scripture of encounter with the Divine, such as Elijah at the cave at Horeb encountering a "sound of sheer silence" following the loud and powerful natural phenomena (1 Kgs. 19:11–13).

3. Robert A. Johnson, *Inner Work: Using Dreams and Active Imagination for Personal Growth* (New York: HarperCollins, 1986), 17.

4. Eugene H. Peterson, *The Message: The Bible in Contemporary Language* (Colorado Springs, CO: NavPress, 2002).

5. One of Flora Slosson Wuellner's imagery meditations brilliantly underscores this capacity of the Divine to heal areas of our unconscious. She offers a depth prayer and meditation in which the meditator imagines that the Christ (or another symbol of the Healer) comes to the entrance to an underground cave, carrying a lamp with a healing light. The meditator asks the Christ to carry the lamp down into the unconscious depths of the cave and to shine the light in areas that need healing, but the meditator stays at the entrance unless he or she is specifically asked by the Christ to go with him to a particular place in the unconscious. The Christ figure is the healer (not us), and the work is done in the unconscious, beyond the meditator's awareness. This was presented as a meditation at the Upper Room Academy, but a version of this prayer can be found in Flora Slosson Wuellner, *Prayer, Stress, and Our Inner Wounds* (Nashville: Upper Room Books, 1985), 35–36.

6. Morton T. Kelsey, *Companions on the Inner Way: The Art of Spiritual Guidance* (New York: Crossroad, 1996), 172–73.

7. For further study in this area, I recommend Thomas Dale Cowan, *Shamanism as a Spiritual Practice for Daily Life* (Berkeley, CA: Crossing Press, 1996). I read Carlos Castenedaʼs books many years ago, but that got me into spiritual trouble for two reasons: drugs, although not necessarily recommended, were often part of the journey, and the focus was on building up "personal power," which could easily lead to ego inflation and self-centeredness. I found this emphasis often in conflict with my Christian spiritual orientation and values.

8. Benedicta Ward, *The Sayings of the Desert Fathers: The Alphabetical Collection*, rev. ed. (Kalamazoo, MI: Cistercian Publications, 1984), xxi–xxiii.

9. Guigo the Carthusian quote submitted by Don H. on Doug Lawrenceʼs website, douglawrence.wordpress.com/2010/02/22/lectio-divina-as-beautifully-sum marised-by-carthusian-prior-guigo/. See also Guigoʼs letter, "The Ladder of Four Rungs," chap. 1, www.umilta.net/ladder.html. This letter contains the first discussion of *lectio divina* in its four-movement form.

10. For instance, one article I found well-written and instructive is by Michael Anne Haywood, "How to Keep a Spiritual Journal," home.earthlink. net/~haywoodm/spiritualjournal.html.

11. See the website for Liberty State Park, www.libertystatepark.com/emma. htm.

12. The traditional term is "write" an icon. Since icons may be regarded as a visual revelatory, equivalent to Scripture, the artist "writes" the icon rather than paints it.

13. The "Trisagion" is one such prayer. Another ancient prayer of this kind is the "Jesus Prayer," which in its longest form reads: "Lord Jesus Christ, Son of God, have mercy on me, a sinner."

14. All of these houses are now open to women and men alike for personal or group retreats.

15. Jason Brian Santos, *A Community Called Taizé: A Story of Prayer, Worship, and Reconciliation* (Downers Grove, IL: InterVarsity Press, 2008), 38.

16. Patricia Garfield, *Creative Dreaming*, rev. ed. (New York: Fireside, 1995). Garfield drew from the anthropological report "Dream Theory in Malaya" by Kilton Stewart when discussing the Senoi Temiar people and their dream culture. That report has drawn a lot of controversy, with critics saying that Stewart fabricated and idealized much of it. Whether or not Stewart was accurate in the portrayal of that culture, the rules for the limited control of situations while in a dream and the ways creative dream products can be elicited, as described by Garfield, stand true to my own experience. I have found that I am capable of following those rules, although often in a limited way, in my dreams. I have also found that I carry the value of those rules into my daily living. Garfieldʼs book also introduced me to the practice of lucid dreaming. Both the Senoi rules for dream control and lucid dreaming offer important ways of engaging the dream state with conscious awareness and control with the aim of bringing a creative product into the waking world.

17.   janphillips.com/shop/story-spinning-harvesting-life-events-harnessing-power/. See Pat Brockman, *The Community Dream: Awakening the Christian Tribal Consciousness* (Boulder, CO: Woven Word Press, 2000), for a description of the project.

18. Prechtel, "To Have the Mind of Christ," app. 2.

19. As I write this I am captured by the possible dream pun on the word "augurs." An augur was an ancient diviner who read signs, such as the flight of birds, as omens. In the dream, it takes some effort to open up the ice (to get past the surface consciousness) and is accomplished by using ice augurs and spoons, which dig through the ice. Getting to the riches (fish) of wisdom takes some effort and requires a willingness to divine the deep truths.

20. Much more information on setting up a dreamwork group or a social dreaming matrix is provided in my book *Where Two or Three Are Gathered*, where I discuss models 5 and 6.

21. See presentations at www.worlddreamspeacebridge.org and its organization's purpose statement. See also Jean Campbell, "What Is Group Dreaming?" *Dream Network Journal* (Spring 2013): 9–10; and Janet Garrett, "The Thesis and the Bridge: The Empathic Nature of Group Dreaming," *Dream Network Journal* (Spring 2013): 24–25.

22. The Book of Common Prayer, 134, 135.

Chapter 4: Contexts for Discernment and Guiding Symbols

1. There are a number of useful works on masculine development. For example, Robert Moore and Douglas Gillette develop the archetypes of the "king, warrior, magician, and lover" (in a book by the same name) as symbols representing the man's psychological capacities that can be immature or develop into maturity, balance, and integration. They claim the same archetypes exist in a woman and speak of the interior "queen" as the regal energy that oversees the realm and makes executive decisions.

2. Lindsey's approach as a biblical literalist and Bible prophecy evangelist was to see apocalyptic stories as coded messages foretelling the end times. There is an urgency in these kind of messages and way of interpretation that denies that this is a literary form that has been reinterpreted many times over the centuries to speak to people who are feeling spiritually (and politically) oppressed. It can be powerfully manipulative to use this as a tool for the supposed prediction of the end time. Such predictions have been offered many times, resulting in failure. I was spiritually needy and it hooked me for a while, but then I learned more about apocalyptic symbolism. It does call us to awaken to the reality of spiritual forces of good and evil and to live spiritually mature lives oriented to God, but no one knows when the "end time" will come (Matt. 24:36, Mark 13:32).

3. The Necronomicon is a mythical book of magic. It first showed up in the fictional writing of H. P. Lovecraft and then gained popular mystique.

4. Thomas Merton, *The Wisdom of the Desert* (New York: New Directions, 1970), 50.

5. English translation by Loren G. Smith, first published in "Flame of Love, Poems of the Spanish Mystics" © 2005 by the Society of St. Paul, Alba House Publications, www.albahouse.org/flame.htm.

6. This kind of group process influenced other groups for discernment, such as the Listening Hearts Ministries model and my spiritual friends model. Variations of the clearness committee as a resource are more often used as part of a discernment and selection process for aspirants for holy orders than in other situations. My hope is that it becomes more widely used for considering other subjects of discernment, both for personal and couples' situations.

7. There are various articles on family meetings easily available online via a simple Web search.

8. Gil Rendle and Alice Mann, *Holy Conversations: Strategic Planning as a Spiritual Practice for Congregations* (Bethesda, MD: Alban Institute, 2003), 24.

9. Prechtel, "To Have the Mind of Christ," 67, 86.

10. Class notes for Dream Matrix Session #4, April 15, 2003.

11. From the video series *The Power of Myth* (*Joseph Campbell with Bill Moyers*), originally broadcast on PBS in 1988.

12. Delivered on the steps of the Lincoln Memorial in Washington, D.C., on August 28, 1963. From Ed Clayton, *Martin Luther King: The Peaceful Warrior* (New York: Pocket Books, 1968).

13. Dwight D. Eisenhower, "Military-Industrial Complex Speech," 1961, coursesa.matrix.msu.edu/~hst306/documents/indust.html.

14. Especially desert father Evagrius Ponticus, and his student John Cassian, adapted the analogy as Christian Neoplatonists.

15. "Asthma and Air Pollution," February 5, 2013, www.arb.ca.gov/research/asthma/asthma.htm.

16. "Climate Change Facts: Answers to Common Questions," www3.epa.gov/climatechange/basics/facts.html.

17. I first heard that phrase "a new covenant with the earth" in the 1990s when the celebrated Anglican preacher and writer, the Rev. Dr. Herbert O'Driskoll, taught biblical themes for preaching at an Episcopal Diocese of Western Michigan clergy conference. His words then, as often has been the case, are proving prophetic.

18. See the National Coalition against Domestic Violence website for current statistics for the nation and by state, www.ncadv.org.

19. See the National Coalition for the Homeless public-policy priorities for 2013, www.nationalhomeless.org/advocacy/PolicyPriorities_2013.html.

20. See "FAQs," National Poverty Center, University of Michigan Gerald R. Ford School of Public Policy, www.npc.umich.edu/poverty.

Additional Guided Meditations and Dream Notes

1. "Sledding Near C," *The World Dream Bank*, www.worlddreambank.org.

2. Patricia Garfield, *Creative Dreaming*, 65–66.

3. www.rollingstone.com/music/news/when-keith-richards-wrote-i-cant-get-no-satisfaction-in-his-sleep-20110509.

4. www.songfacts.com/category-songs_inspired_by_dreams.php.

5. Kelly Bulkeley, *The Wilderness of Dreams: Exploring the Religious Meanings of Dreams in Modern Western Culture* (Albany: State University of New York Press, 1994), 184–86.

6. Jeremy Taylor, *Where People Fly and Water Runs Uphill: Using Dreams to Tap the Wisdom of the Unconscious* (New York: Warner Books, 1992), 5.